Edith Piaf

Her Songs & The Stories Behind Them Translated Into English

Volume Two:

The Decca Years 1947 - 48

The Columbia Years Part 1:1946 - 1954

ISBN: 9798361149117

A catalogue record for this book is available from the British Library.

Also available:

Edith Piaf: Her Songs & The Stories Behind Them Translated Into English:
Volume One: The Polydor Years 1935 - 1945

Part Two of a complete guide to the recorded output of Edith Piaf which includes lyricists, composers, tape recordings, acetates and live recordings of songs not recorded in the studio, and of archived material.

The years 1946 and 1947 are confusing. There was a gap of several months where Piaf was contracted to Decca, but some of the live performances and tape recording of the Decca songs for the radio were archived for many years before being released posthumously by Columbia. The songs are therefore listed in this first section in the order that they were introduced to the public. For a fuller portrait of Piaf's life please refer to my previous books on the subject:

The Piaf Legend, Robson Books, 1988
Piaf, A Passionate Life, Robson Books, 1998
Find Me A New Way To Die: Edith Piaf's Untold Story, Oberon, 2015.
I have included extracts from interviews that I conducted with Serge Reggiani, Michel Emer, Dorothy Squires, Simone Berteaut, Marlene Dietrich, Charles Aznavour and Peggy Lee.

This book is dedicated to the great *chanteuse* Barbara (1930-97), a true friend and inspiration, in this the 25th year of her passing…and *Les enfants de novembre*.

N'oublie pas: la vie sans amis c'est comme un jardin sans fleurs…

Columbia: Period One

1946

Edith Piaf's last visit to a recording studio had been in January 1945, when she had rehearsed—and probably taped or even recorded three songs which would never see the light of day. Much of the rest of this year had been turned over to promoting and launching her latest lover, the Marseille-born crooner Yves Montand (1921-91)—whom she shared with her other lover, the chansonnier Yvon Jeanclaude. In the autumn, all three had been approached to appear in a film—Piaf's third while the other two were yet to cut their acting teeth. Marcel Blistène (1911-91) had worked as an assistant with Paramount since 1930, and *Étoile sans lumière* (Star Without Light) was to be his first vehicle as director. Jeanclaude rejected the offer, and his part was given to Serge Reggiani (1922-2004), remembered as one of the finest singers of his generation, and one of the best-loved. Singing, however, was not his first chosen vocation. Born in Reggio Emilia, Italy, he moved to Paris with his parents in 1930. During the war, while starting out on his career as a stage actor he was a key figure with the Résistance which was probably when he met Piaf. Then, with peacetime, the opportunity came for him to appear in his first film. He recalled:

> Yves Montand was one of my best friends at that time. We were both Italians though we'd spent most

of our lives living in France, and we were just starting out in our acting careers. Piaf had met Yves by way of her agent. He always said that she was in some ways the best thing that had ever happened to him, and in other ways his very worst nightmare.

Piaf never retained a lover for long, once he had served his purpose—mostly, writing songs for her—but she also never dropped one man unless another was waiting in the wings to take his place. Yvon Jeanclaude had been with her since 1941 and was referred to her as her "fuck on demand". As such he had seen off the actors Paul Meurisse and Henri Vidal, and composers Henri Contet and Norbert Glanzberg, though all of these would remain close to Piaf for the rest of her life. Serge recalled what happened, when Jeanclaude refused the part:

> Yves asked Blistène if I could have a part—it was easier in those days. There were no screen tests. If the director thought you were good enough, you got the part. Piaf never let Yves out of her sight for a moment, well aware that Blistène fancied him. For a little while she fixed her sights on me. She always thought ahead—you know, as soon as there were cracks in the relationship, to start looking for a replacement. She and Yves were already having problems. I wasn't interested in her, not in that way, besides which I had nothing to offer her. I wasn't a singer [then], and I wasn't writing songs....I have to

confess that for a novice [sic] she was a tremendous actress. It's sad that she appeared in so few films. She could easily have become the French equivalent of Anna Magnani. *Étoile sans lumière* was a good film, but only because she was in it. It contained too many mistakes.

The "mistakes"—picked up on by the critics—had much to do with the action taking place in 1929, while the clothes, hairstyles, cars, telephones and studio equipment were all from 1945. Despite this the film was a massive success, even in America, which was unusual for a subtitled film. *Étoile sans lumière* would later be remade as *Singin' in the Rain*, with Gene Kelly and Debbie Reynolds. It tells the story of Stella Dora (Mila Parély), a celebrated star from the silent era who is desperate to make the transition to the newly-arrived Talkies, save that she has failed her voice test. She and her team therefore attempt to keep her in the spotlight by duplicitous means. Stella's agent hears his maid, Madeleine (Piaf) singing as she goes about her chores, and decides to take advantage of her. He gets his technician (Reggiani) to record her voice, telling her that she has what it takes to become a famous singer. What she does not know is that her voice will be dubbed over Stella's in a film. When she finally learns the truth during the film's premiere, the agent tries to make amends by offering her an engagement in a music hall. Attempting to sing in front of an audience, she dries up and after a remorseful Stella commits suicide returns to her village to be consoled by her lover, Pierre (Montand), whom we have seen earlier in the film's most famous sequence where they are driving through the country just before their car breaks down.

The five songs were initially taped at the SUF (Société Universelle de Films) studios in January. Four were later recorded for release, Henri Contet and Jean Jal's *C'était une histoire d'amour*—recorded 15 December 1942—was reprised but not re-recorded.

1: *Mariage* (Wedding) (Henri Contet, Marguerite Monnot).
January: soundstage recording for the film soundtrack.
Accompaniment: Guy Luypaerts & His Orchestra.
9 March 1946: tape recording, Radio Suisse-Romande, released posthumously.
Accompaniment: Robert Chauvigny, Marc Bonel, Marc Heyran.
8 October 1947: Columbia DFX 246 A-side. 30cm/12-inch.
26 May 1948: acetate, released posthumously.
18 April 1954: live in French television's *La joie de vivre d'Édith Piaf.*
13 January 1957: live, in French & English, Carnegie Hall, New York.
Accompaniment (1947/1954/1957): Robert Chauvigny & His Orchestra.
The song is performed by Madeleine in *Étoile sans lumière* when, by way of an apology for Stella Dora's behaviour, she is auditioned for a show at the ABC music-hall. In the 1948 version, the lyric is preceded by the tolling of funeral bells.

Six o'clock, Place de la Trinité, when the gun cracked in front of the little café. The lady who had fired looked on in astonishment at the man in grey who had fallen. A number is jotted down in the ledger at the police station. The lady doesn't want to speak, and when the judge is tired, she chats with her past. To think that it all began at the same time as the summer sunshine which seemed set to last—the sunshine which picked out a young man dressed in dark grey who looked like he was made for dancing! So naturally she waltzed [with him], and kissed him afterwards. It takes no more than that to fall in love! A number was jotted down in the register office at the Town Hall in the 14th district. Then everything became wonderful! In beautiful dreams, one can't do better than that…

Finally, when she is alone in her cell, she reflects upon why she killed her husband:

The lady closes her eyes and sees once more, I think, the only day of her life when she made the sign of the Cross. For everything was wondrous. The church sang for them alone. Even the poor man [the bridegroom] was happy! Love was on tour and from high above, the bells rang out full-blast, "*Long live the bride!*" Ring out, bells! He promised to be faithful! Ring out, bells! Your beloved lied! Ring out!

2: *Adieu, mon coeur* (Goodbye, my heart) (Henri Contet, Marguerite Monnot).

January: soundstage recording for the film soundtrack.

23 April: Columbia DF 3069 A-side.

Accompaniment: Guy Luypaerts & His Orchestra.

From the film, *Étoile sans lumière*.

The song, which Piaf never performed on the stage, has to be taken in the context of the film within the film, where at the end of the production, Stella Dora's pirate character has been thrown into prison, while her lover (the "heart" in the song) has been sentenced to death. Thus, chained to the wall in her cell, she laments:

> Goodbye, my heart. You're cast into misfortune. You won't have me watching you die. Goodbye, my heart. Echoes of happiness form sad songs as a way of repentance. In the old days, you breathed in the golden sun. You walked on treasures. We were wanderers. We loved singing. It ends with prisons! Goodbye, my heart. You're cast into misfortune. You won't have me watching you die. Goodbye, my heart. Echoes of happiness form sad songs as a way of repentance.

3: *Le chant du pirate* (The pirate's song) (Henri Contet, Marguerite Monnot).

January: soundtrack recording for the film, with male voice choir.

23 April: Columbia DF 3069 B-side.

Accompaniment: Guy Luypaerts & His Orchestra.

4 June 1946. Tape recording for the radio show *Neuf garçons et une fille chantaient*, released posthumously. Accompaniment: Robert Chauvigny & His Orchestra.

Again, the song has to be taken in the context of the film within the film, wherein Stella Dora's pirate character mimes to Madeleine's voice while at the ship's helm.

> Marching above storms, running through waves and wind, chasing white sailboats. That's us—the fellows in front! That's us pirates—brigands, like our fathers! Heave-ho! Mercy! If you want to string us up, you have to catch us first! Heave-ho! Hoist the Jolly Roger [*pavillon noir* = the pirates' skull-and-crossbows flag]! As long as the wind pushes the frigate along, it's good weather for pirates! As long as the sea's underneath us, it's the pirate who's on top! Heave-ho! Hoist the Jolly Roger! Too bad for your mother's eyes! Too bad for the queen and the king! Too bad if you become a pirate! Jesus was an outlaw! Come visit the stars to sleep in the belly of the sails! Heave-ho! Mercy!

C'est merveilleux, which Madeleine attempts to sing in *Étoile sans lumière*, only to dry up in front of the audience, saw the manipulation tables turned on Piaf for a change, though in the nicest way, as Serge Reggiani recalled:

> Marcel Blistène made her sing that song over and over again, pretending that it had been a bad take. It

hadn't—he just wanted to hear her beautiful singing. But there was also a great deal of tension on the set because the soundtrack had been written by Piaf's former lover, Henri Contet. He visited the set every day and when Piaf saw how much this was annoying Yves, she started flirting with Contet. Yves exacted his revenge by spending the night with his old flame, Reda Caire. This didn't bother Piaf. She called Yvon Jean-Claude, a singer she had been involved with a few years earlier. They were in bed the next night at her hotel when Yves came banging on the door. Yvon was forced to hide in the wardrobe for hours, stark naked, until Piaf and Yves had finished making love and were asleep. Then he escaped through the window. Life was so complicated in those days!

4: *C'est merveilleux* (It's wonderful) (Henri Contet, Marguerite Monnot).
January: soundtrack recording for the film.
28 April: Columbia DF 3170 A-side.
Accompaniment: Guy Luypaerts & His Orchestra.
This is the song that Madeleine sings while driving through the countryside with her lover (Yves Montand).

> The day you met me was overwhelmingly sad, my thoughts dragging around an endless boredom. But your arrival was enough for me to forget my pains. It's wonderful, being together. Joy watches over us.

It's wonderful, being in love. Life is painted in heavenly hues [*la vie est peinte en bleue*] with big strokes of sunshine! Since I love you, and you love me—it's wonderful! We'll spend all our lives singing about so great a love. For such a lovely song, life doesn't have enough days. We'll make a harmony that will never end! It's wonderful when you're in love—waking up to beautiful days! Since you love me, and I love you, it's wonderful!

5: *Dans ma rue* (In my street) (Jacques Datin)
8 March: tape recording, Radio Suisse-Romande. Released posthumously.
Piano accompaniment: Robert Chauvigny.
Jacques Datin (1920-73) later collaborated with his partner Maurice Vidalin (1924-86) on hits for Juliette Gréco, Marcel Amont, Barbara and many others. One of their most celebrated songs was *Nous les amoureux*, with which Jean-Claude Pascal won the Eurovision Song Contest in 1961. This lengthy one tells the woeful tale of the girl who is forced into prostitution by her drunken father.

I live in a corner of Old Montmartre. My father comes home drunk every evening. To feed the four of us, my poor mother works in the laundry. I'm ill. I stay at the window, watching people from other parts of town passing by. When the day's over, there are things that make me a little afraid. In my street there are people walking about. I hear them in

12

the night, whispering. When I'm lulled to sleep by a song, I'm awakened suddenly by screams—whistles blowing, footsteps dragging back and forth. Then silence, which makes my heart go all cold. In my street, shadows walk around. I tremble—I'm cold and afraid. My father told me one day, *"My girl, you can't stay there* [at the window] *for ever. You're a good-for-nothing—that runs in the family. You've got to earn your crust. Men find you rather pretty. All you have to do is go out on an evening. Lots of women earn a living working their beat!"*

Thus, the girl becomes a prostitute, though apparently not a very enterprising one, and in her depression and delirium concludes:

For weeks and weeks I have no home, no money. I don't know how the others manage, but I'm unable to find a customer. I beg alms from passers-by. A little bread, a little warmth. But I'm not bold enough, and now it's me who makes *them* afraid! In my street, I walk around every evening. People hear me sobbing in the night. The wind sings to the sky. My whole body's chilled by the rain. I can't do this anymore. I endlessly wait for the good Lord to come and invite me to warm myself next to Him! In my street there are angels who take me away, for ever. My nightmare is over...

6: *Un refrain courait dans la rue* (A song ran through the street) (Edith Piaf, Robert Chauvigny).

9 March 1946: tape recording, Radio Suisse-Romande for the "last-minute" broadcast, *Entrée Libre*.

Accompaniment: Robert Chauvigny, Marc Bonel, Marc Heyran.

4 January 1947: Columbia DF 3152 B-side.

Accompaniment: Guy Luypaerts & His Orchestra.

16 March 1947: tape recording, Radio Suisse-Romande, released posthumously.

Accompaniment: Robert Chauvigny, Bonel, Heyran.

October 1947: studio recording for the soundtrack of the film, *Neuf Garçons, un cœur*.

Accompaniment: Guy Luypaerts & His Orchestra.

> In love you must have pride—to know when to shut up, how to have dignity, to know the right moment to leave, to hide your pain with a smile. And I told myself while walking that I'd known how to leave on time. Though my heart was despairing, he wouldn't have seen me crying. A refrain ran through the street, jostling the passers-by. It slipped through the throng with an engaging melody. I was in its path. It stopped before me and told me to be wise. *"You're sad! My God, why! Come on—get inside my song! There are handsome boys! Throw your sadness into the gutter water and turn your back on him!"*

She then addresses the song:

> "*Your verse must be cheerful! Let's talk about the month of May, the trees clothed in lilacs, and the summer in full-swing! There are violets—a balcony. An old poet's singing a song! My dress is faded by the sunshine!* [The sunshine] *keeps me awake!*"

She continues, reflecting the effect that the refrain had on others within the crowd:

> A refrain ran through the street, jostling the passers-by with an engaging little tune. People in its path looked on with surprise, stopping their chatter. "*What's this boorish thing?*" "*Yes, but the tune's catchy and the words engaging!*" Moreover, within [the refrain] there was laughter at close range.

And she offers advice to others who may feel the way she once did:

> If this refrain running through the street can chase away your torments, then get into the crowd. There's room, if you push!

The nine-strong Compagnons de la Musique, who specialised in obscure folk songs performed in antiquated French, had formed in 1941, and had bumped into Piaf while she had been touring the German camps. In February

1946, they had changed their name to Les Compagnons de la Chanson, and at around this time they appeared with Piaf in a gala in Paris. For her and the leader of the troupe, Jean-Louis Jaubert (1920-2013), it was love at first sight. Yvon Jeanclaude and Yves Montand were retained for a little while, but by early April they were no longer her lovers. Because Piaf had thus far refused to record *Mariage* in the studio, Columbia did not have a song to put on the B-side of the recording. She suggested one by Les Compagnons: *Margolan va t'a l'iau*, a ditty arranged by Francis Poulenc about a maiden who goes to the stream to collect water, and falls in.

In the meantime, a deal was struck between Columbia and the Disney Studios in the United States. *Make Mine Music*, comprising ten animated segments, had been released on 20 April. The performers included Benny Goodman, Jerry Colonna, Dinah Shore, Sterling Holloway and the Andrews Sisters. It was decided that for the French release, *La boîte à musique*, scheduled to be premiered on 28 September, the American artistes would be overdubbed by French ones. These included Renée Lebas and André Dassary with Piaf and Les Compagnons overdubbing the Andrews Sisters' 7-minutes segment.

7: *Johnny Fedora et Alice Bonnet-Bleu* (Johnny Fedora and Alice Blue Bonnet) (Jacques Plante, Marc Lanjean, Allie Wrubel, Charles Wolcott).
May: soundtrack recording for *La boite a musique*. Released posthumously.

21 May 1954: segment released in French cinemas.

The story is that of two hats in a department store window who fall in love, only to be separated when Alice is sold. To fully understand the song, one has to watch the footage as Johnny despairs while searching for her, though all ends happily when they meet again by chance.

Alice and Johnny, that's what they were called, in the window of the department store. A handsome man's hat and a little blue bonnet placed next to him, by chance. He serenades her [*lui chante des romances*] while dreaming of a huge cardboard box where they can live together. But bad luck enters the equation—had to happen sooner or later. The lady's hat is sold on promotion for 35 francs 75 cents! "*Johnny, oh, Johnny, your little Blue Bonnet leaves with tears in her eyes! But stay confident. With hope, all will turn out well in the end!*"

Thus Johnny becomes disheartened. He escapes from the department store window and goes off in search of his beloved, imagining that he is seeing her amongst the crowds, while a voice tells him:

"*Johnny, oh Johnny! Perhaps your little Blue Bonnet has gone to some other paradise! But stay confident! With hope, all will turn out well in the end!*" The days pass, and he trudges along, his soul weary, sometimes returning to the department store battered and dishevelled. Rolling along the pavement, poor Johnny has lost all hope. His beautiful Alice will never hear him again. His sweet dream is over...

And then, the miracle occurs!

An ice-cream deliveryman—and, sitting on the mane of one of his horses is Alice, with such a beautiful expression! *"Johnny oh Johnny! And you, dear Blue-Bonnet are reunited! You remained confident and, with hope, your dreams will always be heavenly!"*

In May, Piaf was cast as the murderess-turned-smuggler Madame Rose in the film *Macadam* (UK: The Backstreets of Paris). Her co-star was ex-lover Paul Meurisse, and the production was co-directed by her friend Marcel Blistène and Jacques Feyder. A score was requisitioned and the title-track recorded, but Piaf was replaced at the last moment by Feyder's wife, Françoise Rosay. To show that there were no hard feelings, Piaf taped the song, and also sang it at the film's premiere. She then insisted that it be given to her friend, Marianne Michel, who recorded it.

8: *Macadam* (Henri Contet, Marguerite Monnot).
May: soundtrack recording for the film, archived.
August: acetate, listed with Éditions Arpège and also with Éditions Paul Beuscher, archived.

26 November: live performance, Cinéma Balzac, never released.

9: *Miss Otis regrette* (Miss Otis regrets) (Cole Porter, Louis Hennevé, Louis Palex).
4 June: tape recording for the radio show *Neuf garçons et une fille chantaient*, released posthumously.
Piano accompaniment: Robert Chauvigny.
Introduced by Douglas Byng in *Hi Diddle Diddle* at London's Savoy Theatre in October 1934. One month later, Suzy Solidor recorded the French adaptation, the lyrics closely adhering to the originals. Controversial at the time, it tells of a reversal of roles—the lynching of a white woman who has murdered her unfaithful lover—when lynching victims were usually African-American males. Louis Hennevé (Houzeau, 1885-1972) and Louis Palex (Paul Ganne) famously provided the French lyrics to Vernon Duke and Yip Harburg's *April in Paris*.

> Miss Otis regrets she's unable to dine today, Madame! For yesterday, she went into the woods and wandered into Lovers' Lane…When she realised that her beautiful love affair was over, she ran towards the man who had indignantly betrayed her. From her Chinese velvet dress she took out a Browning, Madame, and killed him without hesitation. Miss Otis regrets she's unable to dine. The crowd came, broke into the prison and seized her, Madame. They dragged her to the old lime tree,

where they hanged her. And just before passing away, she lifted her lovely head and murmured, "Miss Otis regrets she's unable to dine!"

10: *Monsieur est parti en voyage* (Monsieur has gone on a trip) (Jacques Larue, Michael Carr).
4 June: tape recording for the radio show *Neuf garçons et une fille chantaient*, released posthumously.
Piano accompaniment: Robert Chauvigny.
Written in 1937 for Marie Dubas (1894-1972), Piaf's favourite entertainer. Jacques Larue (1906-61) worked often with Piaf. Among the more famous compositions of Leeds-born Michael Carr (1905-68) were *We're Going to Hang Out the Washing on The Siegfried Line* and *South of the Border*. This song, which makes little sense, appears to tell the story of the mistress who turns up at her lover's place to ask for money he owes her, only to find him gone.

If your love-affairs sing victorious, my friends, I envy you. My own is but a simple story—the story of my life. Imagine, for one second, a maid telling you, *"Monsieur's gone on a trip, and he's left nothing for you! No, Madame, I'm not leading you on. I know nothing more than that. Nothing was said about a meeting! Monsieur simply gave me the responsibility* [m'a chargé tout simplement], *if a lady required him after he left the apartment, of telling her he was very sorry. Alas, Monsieur had to pay me wages not knowing when he'd be returning.*

Yesterday, while he was packing, he appeared to me to be crying...There's no question of him meeting you!" And if this story's too sad—well, my friends, forget it! Nothing exists in my own life since that horrible day. And when my heart gets too tender, each time I think I hear, *"Monsieur's gone on a trip. He left nothing for you!"*

11: *Dans les prisons de Nantes* (In the prisons of Nantes) (Traditional, arranged by Marc Herrand).
4 June: tape recording for the radio show *Neuf garçons et une fille chantaient*, released posthumously.
26 June: Columbia DF 3053 A-side.
A cappella with Les Compagnons. Fred Mella solo.
Marc Herrand (Marc Holtz, b.1925) was a co-founder and member of Les Compagnons. He left the group in 1952 to marry the singer Yvette Giraud. In this, the first line of each stanza is repeated. Fred Mella (1924-2014) was the group's lead singer. In parts of the song Piaf becomes the jailor's daughter, Mella the prisoner who commits suicide.

PIAF: In the prisons of Nantes, there's a prisoner that no one sees except the jailor's daughter. She brings him something to eat and drink, and white shirts when he wants to change.
MELLA: One day, he asks, *"What are they saying about me?"*
PIAF: They're saying all over town that you're going to die, tomorrow.

MELLA: Since I must die, untie my feet.
PIAF: The girl was a youngster. She freed his feet.
MELLA: Wide awake, the gallant man jumped into the Loire.
PIAF: All the bells in Nantes started ringing.

12: *Les trois cloches* (The three bells) (Gilles).
Sung *a cappella* with Les Compagnons de la Chanson.
4 June 1946. Taped for the radio show *Neuf garçons et une fille chantaient*, released posthumously.
25 June: Columbia DCX 76 (France, Holland, UK); DFX 242 (France, second pressing); CQX 16629 (Italy); DNX 27 (Norway); 10054 (Canada) A-side, 30cm/12-inch.
Perrine était servant (Perrine was a servant), performed by Les Compagnons, was on each B-side.
1947: soundstage recording for *Neuf garçons, un coeur.*
14 May 1956: live, *La joie de vivre Edith Piaf.*
1 March 1961: tape recording, released posthumously.
Piaf's first multinational release. Later recorded in English, when Jean-Francois Nicot became Jimmy Brown.
Gilles was the pseudonym of the French-Swiss actor and *chansonnier* Jean Villard (1895-1982), one half (with Aman-Julien Maistre) of the Gilles & Julien duo.

LCDLC: Village, deep in the valley, as if lost, almost ignored. Here, in the starry night, a new-born is given to us. His name is Jean-François Nicot. He's chubby, sweet and pink. Tomorrow at the church, handsome little man, you'll be baptised.

PIAF: A bell rings. Its voice echoes, telling the astonished world that it's for Jean-François Nicot. It's to welcome a soul, a flower which opens to the day, barely a flame, still feeble claiming protection, tenderness, love.

LCDLC: Village, deep in the valley, far from the roads, far from humanity. Here, after nineteen years, his heart in turmoil, Jean-François takes the sweet Elise, white as apple-blossom, to be his wife. Before God, in the old church, they are married.

PIAF: All the bells are ringing. Their voices echo, wonderfully proclaiming the wedding of Jean-François Nicot. *"One heart, one soul!"* says the priest. *"Always retain the pure flame which rises and proclaims the greatness of your love!"*

LCDLC: Village, deep in the valley. Days, nights, time has flown by. Here, in the starry night a heart sleeps, François has died. For all flesh is like the grass, the flower in the fields. Cobs, ripe fruits, bouquets and wreaths. Alas, everything is withered [*desséchant*].

PIAF: A bell rings. It sings in the wind, haunting and monotonous. It says again to the living, *"Do not tremble, faithful hearts! One day, God will make a sign. Under His wing you will find eternal life, the eternity of love!"*

13: *Céline* (Traditional, arranged Marc Herrand).
26 June: Columbia DF 3053 B-side.

Sung *a cappella* with Les Compagnons de la Chanson.
The group perform the entire song, with Piaf joining in for the penultimate refrain. As with the previous item, many of the lines are repeated.

> LCDLC: There are three young boys leaving for the war, all missing their mistresses—the youngest of the three missing his a lot, and rightly so. She was the prettiest girl around! The good soldier goes to find his captain. *"Hello, my Captain! Give me leave so that I can go and see Céline, who does nothing but weep!"* The captain replies, like any man of war, *"Here's your road-map and passport. Go see your sweetheart. You'd go, anyhow!"* The gallant one goes to his father's castle. *"Hello, Father! Hello, Mother—brothers and dear relations, not forgetting Céline, whom my heart loves so much!"* His father replies, *"But your Céline is dead! She died, calling for you! Her body's in the ground, her soul in heaven!"* So the gallant one goes to weep over her grave. *"Céline—my Céline, speak to me! My heart despairs, not seeing you anymore!"* Celine replies…
> PIAF: *My mouth is filled with earth…yours is filled with love! I still cherish the hope of seeing you again, one day!"*
> LCDLC: The good soldier goes to find his captain. *"Hello, my Captain. I'm back, since Céline is dead. I'll serve forever!"*

14: *Le roi a fait battre tambour* (The king made the drums beat) (Traditional, arranged Marc Herrand).

17 July: Columbia BF 146 A-side.

Sung *a cappella* with Les Compagnons de la Chanson.

Ukraine (Jacques Larue, Alex Siniavine) performed by Les Compagnons without Piaf, was on the B-side.

1949: re-issue, B-side of second pressing of Piaf's *Paris*.

The song, wherein lines are regularly repeated, recalls an incident between the King and the Marquis.

> The King made the drums beat, to see all his ladies. And the first one he saw delighted his soul. *"Tell me, Marquis, do you know her? Who is this lovely lady?"* And the Marquis replied, *"Sire, she's my wife!"* *"Marquis, you're happier than me, having such a lovely lady! If you want to give her to me, I'll look after her!"* *"Sire, if you weren't the King, I would take revenge. But, since you're the King, to your obedience!"* *"Marquis, don't get angry. In my armies, I'll appoint you Marshall of France!"*

Then we hear the response from the lady herself:

> *"Farewell, my beloved! Farewell, my heart! Farewell my hope! Since you have to serve the king, let us separate!"*

And the Queen has her revenge by having the Marquis' wife poisoned!

The Queen had a bouquet made—lovely lilies. And the scent of this bouquet killed the Marquise!

15: *Quand je te vois danser* (When I see you dancing) (Edith Piaf, Paul Durand).
August: possible acetate. Listed with Éditions Arpège and also with Éditions Paul Beuscher.
No other details.

16: *La Complainte du roi Renaud* (The Lament of King Renaud) (Traditional, arranged Marc Herrand).
9 October: acetate, released posthumously.
The recorded version comprises around two-thirds of the traditional lyrics, which would have fit on a 30cm/12-inch recording. Piaf and Les Compagnons performed the full version on stage, running to around seven minutes, making more sense than what is recorded. The sections not included on the recording are marked [[…]]. The verses are performed by Les Compagnons, who take on the roles of the King and his mother trying to pull the wool over the eyes of the naïve Queen, who has just given birth, and whose lines are sung by Piaf.

King Renaud came back from the war carrying his guts in his hand. His mother was on the battlements, and saw her son Renaud returning.

MOTHER: Renaud, Renaud! Rejoice! Your wife's given birth to a King!

RENAUD: I cannot rejoice, for my mother or for my son! Come on, Mother. Go ahead—prepare me a beautiful white bed!

[[I won't stay long, here. At midnight I will pass away. Let me lie down here, where she who has given birth cannot hear!]]

And at midnight, King Renaud gave up the ghost.

[[Morning came and the grooms were weeping. They were still weeping at lunchtime.]]
[[QUEEN: Tell me, Mother-in-Law. Why are the grooms weeping?]]
[[MOTHER: My girl, while bathing the horses, they allowed the most beautiful one to drown.]]
[[QUEEN: But why, Mother-in-Law, do they weep so much for a horse? When Renaud comes home, he'll bring the most beautiful horse! And tell me, Mother-in-Law. Why are the servants weeping?]]
[[MOTHER: My girl, while washing the shrouds, they ruined the best one!]]
[[QUEEN: But Mother-in-Law—why are they weeping because of a shroud? When Renaud returns, he'll bring back the most beautifully embroidered shroud!]]

QUEEN: Tell me, Mother-in-Law. What's that noise that I hear?

MOTHER: My girl, that's the carpenters sawing planks of wood.

QUEEN: But tell me, Mother-in-Law. What are the priests chanting?

MOTHER: My girl, that's the procession going around the house.

[[Noon comes, and she is getting ready for Mass]].

QUEEN: Tell me, Mother-in-Law. Which dress shall I wear today? The white one, or the grey one?

MOTHER: The black one would be a better choice.

QUEEN: But tell me, Mother-in-Law. What does the black one signify?

MOTHER: For a woman who's taking care of a baby, black is more suitable.

She entered the church, and was given a candle, and while kneeling saw fresh earth under his bench.

QUEEN: Tell me, Mother-in-Law. Why is there fresh earth?

MOTHER: My girl, I can't hide it from you any more. Renaud is dead and buried.

[[QUEEN: Renaud, Renaud, my comfort! Here you are in the ranks of the dead!]]

QUEEN: And if King Renaud is dead, take the key to my treasure-chest! Take my rings and my jewels!

Feed my son Renaud well. Earth, open up! Earth, split open so that I can go to Renaud, my King!

The earth opens up! The earth splits open and swallows the beautiful one!

17: *Et elle chantait* (And she sang) (Henri Contet, Marguerite Monnot).
3 October: tape recording, Radio Suisse-Romande.
12 January 1947: acetate, archived.
Both versions sung *a cappella* with Les Compagnons de la Chanson, both released posthumously.
Les Compagnons sing the often confusing and frequently meaningless lyrics, while Piaf, singing vocalese, augments the chorus.

The girl in blue who comes and goes in the song that I'm singing for you had no roof, no fire, nothing but the sky for a roof. You heard her laughing and singing on the roads, on the hills, stealing fruit from orchards when the bells called [the workers] to Mass. She sang for the wind that battered her, for the sunshine that burned her. All along the highways, her hair bleached, her arms bathed in light, intoxicated by the sound of the bells, she sang. But for a boy from the North, who came here for the fruit-picking, she changed her ways. Goodbye, songs! He took her to his home far away from the roads, and it was said how she would never sing again on the highways. But four walls is too much for a child of the stars and the strong wind coming from up above, to prevent her from being so pale. For him, love came first. But the girl in blue was dying of boredom, and to forget him headed barefoot back to the hills where everyone sang, where music rustled in the foliage and the wind laughed along the roads. The wind sang, and from leaf to root, the song of the wind passed wherever she sang. Singing, the girl marched to the music, and beneath the footsteps of the child a hymn flowed. She sang, her voice rising, echoing, sounding along the roads. She sang, and everything bloomed as she passed by all along the roads.

18: *Je m'en fous pas mal* (I really don't care) (Michel Émer).
9 October: Columbia DFX 244 B-side. 30cm/12-inch.
Accompaniment: Guy Luypaerts & His Orchestra.
16 March 1947: tape recording, Radio Suisse-Romande, released posthumously.
Accompaniment: Robert Chauvigny, Marc Bonel, Marc Heyran.
December 1948: live, Copacabana Club, broadcast 20 June 1949, French radio, and also by the BBC as part of their *Rendezvous in Paris* series.
Accompaniment: Daniel White & His Orchestra.
Some sources claim the Copacabana recital was broadcast live in June 1949 and not previously recorded. The fact that

the orchestra introduces Piaf on to the stage with *White Christmas* dictates otherwise. Bandleader-actor Daniel White (1912-97) was born in Paris but raised in West Yorkshire, England. During World War II he worked as an interpreter with the British forces and was badly injured during the evacuation of Dunkirk, his bravery very much impressing Piaf. She later sang this song in English, minus the verses, as *I Shouldn't Care*, where it took on a new meaning entirely.

I was born in the Passage de la Bonne Graine [literal translation: Good-Seed Alley]. I've been taking the seed for a long time. I work like a dog all week. I swear to you, the boss is happy! My friends got angry [and said], *"It's not very smart, what you're doing there! What you're doing has to be done, but one day you'll regret it!"* I really don't care. Anything could happen to me, but I really don't care! My Sundays are my own. Maybe it's a cliché, but it makes no difference to me. I don't care! There are the banks of the Seine, the avenue de l'Opéra. There's the Bois de Vincennes—what a beautiful Sunday is to be had there! Then there's the dance-hall which gives me the chills. There are stars more beautiful than jewels—handsome men who kiss you on the neck. As for the rest, I don't care!

She remembers the dancehall where she found the man of her dreams:

It was on one of those wonderful Sundays that the two of us started dancing. Big dark eyes, long white hands. So I let him kiss me. My friends got angry [and said], "*Everyone knows this bloke is heartless. He's an arsehole, a wretch who will soon reveal his true colours!*" I really don't care. Anything could happen to me, but I really don't care! I have my own lover! Maybe it's a cliché, but it makes no difference to me. I don't care! There's his arms that embrace me. There's his body, soft and warm—his mouth that kisses me! My lover's *so* handsome! Then there's the dancehall. When I'm in his arms, it's crazy. I'd be wrong [to refuse] when he says, "Come on, let's go home!" The animal! I'd go anywhere with him. As for the rest, I don't care!

But, this being a Piaf love-story, all does not end well:

I lived through such wonderful moments when he was holding me in his arms. I never believed that one could be happy in life until that point. Then one day, when all was going so well [*où tout n'était que rires*]—one spring day filled with joy, he left without saying a word. Without even kissing me goodbye for a last time.

Even so, she has no regrets:

I really don't care. Anything could happen to me—

but I really don't care! I have my past. Maybe it's a cliché but it makes no difference to me. I don't care. The memories surrounding me sing deep within my heart, and each place I pass reminds me of my joy. Then there's the dancehall. I dance, I close my eyes, and pretend we're still together. Sometimes, it hurts. My heart beats wildly. It makes no difference to me. I don't care!

19: *Le petit homme* (The little man) (Henri Contet, Marguerite Monnot).
9 October: Columbia DFX 244 A-side 30 cm/12-inch.
Accompaniment: Guy Luypaerts & His Orchestra.
16 March 1947: tape recording, Radio Suisse-Romande, released posthumously.
Accompaniment: Robert Chauvigny, Marc Bonel, Marc Heyran.
Piaf later recorded an English version, *One Little Man*, in an almost word-for-word adaptation.

There was everyone going about their daily routine. There was heckling at the crossroads, and people buying their newspapers, and all those taking the Métro. There was a parade on the boulevards, the sales-pitch of the gossipy old street-hawker. And the April sun, reflected in the dirty water of the *ruisseaux* [*ruisseaux* translates as streams, but in this instance the water which runs along a typical Parisian gutter]. There was a little man, going along his way. Nobody much, the little man with his old threadbare coat. But he had a mistress who cost him a lot of money. She sold him her beautiful youth, and caresses he paid for with cash. There was his Saturday night life—the staircase and the corridor. There was the door at the end, then two arms around his neck. There were the flowers on the piano, the whiteness of the curtains. Then there were the hours spent on the big blue couch. All of these things made him happy.

This being a typical Piaf song however, the little man's joy is short-lived:

There was the locked door, the note pushed underneath. Pretty paper edged with roses telling him things he didn't understand at first. A little man who's abandoned. Nothing to do but go away into the cold street where everything is buzzing—and with no one, all alone, so that he can weep better. There was everyone going about their business, the usual fanfare. Waltzes, playing on phonograms, burst out of the bistros. There was a boy singing, and a girl laughing. All the wonders of love! And the little man weeping in the middle of it all.

Étoile sans lumière with Serge Reggiani…

…and with Yves Montand.

On stage, singing *Mariage*.

The role that was not to be.

1947

Piaf told the story of how, in 1945, she was sitting in a restaurant with her friend, Marianne Michel, when an idea came into her head for a song—of how she had taken a lipstick from her handbag and scribbled the words to *Les choses en roses* (Things in pink) on the tablecloth. Michel, who had already performed several Piaf rejects, suggested that the title be amended to *La vie en rose* (Life in pink). Piaf, who also wrote the music, was not yet a member of S.A.C.E.M. ((Société des Auteurs, Compositeurs et Éditeurs de Musique), which required passing an exam, therefore others had to countersign her work. Marguerite Monnot refused, denouncing it as inferior, and Louiguy (Louis Guglielmi, 1916-91), who had countersigned Piaf's other work, accepted responsibility for this one which was deposited with S.A.C.E.M. in November 1945. Michel recorded it in 1946. In those days, the unwritten law of the French music-hall was that a song remained the property of whoever recorded it first for a six-month period. Piaf had always ignored the rule, creating no small amount of animosity with the "enemy"—currently Lucienne Delyle and Renée Lebas. With *La vie en rose*, she allowed Marianne Michel her moment of glory, though her recording of the song did not sell well. The Piaf version, on the other hand, proved the biggest success in her career so far. Reaching Number 23 in the *Billboard* chart, it was the first French recording to sell more than a million copies in the United States.

20: *La vie en rose* (Life in rose) (Edith Piaf, Louiguy).
4 January: Columbia DF 3152 A-side:
Accompaniment: Guy Luypaerts & His Orchestra.
March: soundstage recording for the film, *Neuf Garçons, un cœur*.
Un refrain courait dans la rue (Item **#6**), introduced the previous year and recorded in the same session, was on the B-side.

> Eyes which make me lower my own, a laugh that is lost on his mouth. That's the untouched portrait of the man I belong to! When he takes me in his arms, he whispers to me—I see life in pink [aka life through rose-tinted glasses]. He tells me words of love—everyday words, and that does something to me. A piece of joy has entered my heart, and I know what caused it! It's him for me, me for him, for life! He told me this, swore it for life! And as soon as I see him, I feel my heart beating inside me! Nights of endless love, a great happiness has taken hold. Troubles and sorrows fade away, happy to die! When he takes me in his arms...I see life in pink! *"It's you for me, me for you—for life!"* he told me, swore it for life! And as soon as I see him, I feel my heart beating inside me!

21: *Sérénade Florentine* (Jacques Plante, Louiguy).
Possible tape recording, no other details.
Registered and deposited with the S.A.C.E.M. on the same

day as *La vie en rose*, and subsequently recorded by Pierre Malar (Louis Azum, 1924-2013) who specialised in exotic songs, and who had been discovered and launched by Piaf and Henri Contet in 1944, just after the Liberation.

22: *Le rideau tombe avant la fin* (The curtain falls before the end) (Jean-Marc Thibault, Jacques Besse).
6 January: tape recording, Radio Suisse-Romande, released posthumously.
Accompaniment: Guy Luypaerts & His Orchestra.
Jacques Besse (1921-99) was a composer of film scores whose best-known work was for Yves Allegret's *Dédée d'Anvers* (1948). Piaf had recorded his *Un monsieur me suit dans la rue* in January 1944. Jean-Marc Thibault (1923-2017) was one half of the celebrated comedy duo, Pierre et Thibault, with Roger Pierre. A grim song, at five minutes it is one of Piaf's longest and hysterical in parts.

> The curtain falls before the end of the third act. Fine exits [deaths] for actors aren't of much interest. At times, life starts off well. When it starts off badly, we just get on with it. But in the end, we can't do anything about it. The curtain falls before the end. All the locals who knew him, including me, could tell you, *"The first thing you see is his smile. They don't make blokes like that anymore!"* Of course, the others were jealous. But that's not important. He carried good luck around with him. He was the one who always won at poker as in love. Always happy,

always content, he should have lived to be a hundred. Even so, it was me that he wanted, even though there was so much difference between his good luck and my misfortune. Perhaps that's what pleased him—having too much happiness, he wanted to share it. But he retained the upper hand. Perhaps he didn't have a heart? He said, *"I'm like the statues. People hurt themselves when they hit me. No one's ever been able to tame me!"* It was wrong of me to be tempted! The curtain falls before the end...We're surrounded by clever people who know how to control their destiny. The whole world belongs to them, so long as they're play-acting. They forget there's nothing we can do about it, that the curtain falls before the end. I didn't know how to enjoy his riches, how to make the best of his good luck. I wanted to hurt him a little—he was too rich, too strong! When he saw me in a dancehall with a bloke of no importance, he said, *"My good luck's ended—that's the first time anyone's made me feel bad!"* I didn't know that he wanted to kill himself, or if it was bad luck that had mixed him up. They found him early one morning, his beautiful jalopy at the bottom of a ravine. Deaths like that are pointless. They don't interest Fate! I no longer believe in early mornings. Night always falls too quickly and Fate promises nothing. The curtain falls before the end!

Immediately after this session, Piaf travelled to Brussels to complete her obligation with Decca, as detailed in the next segment of this book. Returning to Paris, she made her fourth film, *Neuf garcons, un Coeur*, with Les Compagnons de la Chanson. Directed by Georges Freedland (1910-93), it was filmed over a period of just twelve days at the Billancourt Studios, and with a limited budget. A fantasy set one Christmas Eve, it tells the story of Christine (Piaf), the leader of a hard-up group of singers (Les Compagnons) who are starving and desperate to find work. First she falls asleep and dreams that she is in heaven, where she is befriended by The Boss (Marcel Vallée) who appropriately runs a nightclub called Paradise. Needless to say, with the help of The Boss, all ends well.

The film's premiere, set for October, was delayed when Piaf and the group signed independent contracts to appear in separate nightclubs in New York. Meanwhile, and ahead of a short season at the Étoile, they embarked on a tour of Greece—a near-disaster because the country was embroiled in a general election campaign. By now, Piaf's relationship with Jean-Louis Jaubert had started to cool, and she enjoyed a "holiday romance" with a temperamental young actor, Takis Menelas (Dimitris Horn, 1921-98). The affair might have progressed further had Menelas not asked her to give up her career and marry him. She would never have agreed to the former, of course, and when she found out that Menelas already *had* a wife, he was dumped. He subsequently would be featured in two songs—*Si tu partais* and *Un homme comme les autres.*

23: *Qu'as tu fait, John?* (Michel Émer)

6 October: acetate, prohibited from release, believed to have been destroyed, but subsequently relocated in the Columbia archives and released posthumously.

Accompaniment: Marius Coste & His Orchestra.

December 1948: live performance, Copacabana, Paris. Released posthumously.

Accompaniment: Daniel White & His Orchestra.

24 December 1956: live performance, Porte St-Jean, Quebec. Released posthumously.

Accompaniment: Robert Chauvigny & His Orchestra.

Piaf's third song championing the Negro slave: the others are *Le grand voyage du pauvre nègre* (1938) and *Jimmy, c'est lui* (1940), and her second about a lynching—in this instance brought about by a white woman who allows the black man to hang because he refused her advances. While performing the song on stage, Piaf emulated the snapping of John's neck by grabbing a drumstick and breaking it over her knee. She was prohibited from doing this after a recital in Quebec in 1956 when several women fainted in the audience, and subsequently removed the song from her repertoire. Piaf's regular orchestra leaders (Luypaerts, Chauvigny, Normand) refused to have anything to do with it, so she chose Marius Coste (d.1960), who had arranged the French version of Dorothy Squires' *The Gypsy*, for Yvon Jeanclaude. The recording was thought to have been destroyed but was found in the Columbia archives after Piaf's death. She was not permitted to sing any of the above songs in America.

Under a blazing sun, near the Savanna in the heart of Louisiana, John works in a big cotton field. He is sweating profusely—he's hot, can't take it any more. Then suddenly a crowd [a lynch mob] comes running along the road towards poor John, who is shaking. Margaret raises her finger, and tells the gathering, *"He forced himself on me!"*

Then the people yell at him, and at each other:

"What have you done, John? What have you done?"
"He forced himself on a white woman!"
"Sunday—he drank too much, got himself pissed!"

And, finally:

They took John to the village, to the sheriff's house. All the white people screaming with rage, demanding hasty judgement. *"He's a bastard! Let's hang him! Drag him out of his cell and string him up to teach him a lesson!"* John wriggles on the branch—a shudder, and it's all over. White men and white women can sleep on a night! *"What have you done, John? What have you done? You mustn't touch white women! You look all done in, at the end of your branch. You've been hanged—a job well done!"*

Then we learn that *John* who was the victim, not Margaret:

43

The house where everyone's asleep—Margaret banging hard [on the door]. The sheriff wakes up and asks her, "*What do you want?*" She tells him, "*I'm the one who desired the Negro. I've come to accuse myself! I was in love with the Negro, but John rejected me!*" The sheriff's angry. "*All this fuss about a Negro! Don't worry about it, Margaret! Goodnight!*"

And the song concludes:

"*What have you done, John—rejecting a white woman? There you are, hanging from a branch!*" And a voice replies in the wind, "*He's happier than before! John's in heaven, where poor Negros pray! John's now very joyful! He's at the right hand of God!*"

24: *C'est pour ça* (That's why) (Henri Contet, Marguerite Monnot).
March: soundstage recording for *Neuf garcons, un coeur.*
7 October: Columbia DFX 247 A-side.
28 July 1948: acetate, released posthumously.
Accordion accompaniment (all three): Marc Bonel.
Sung with Les Compagnons de la Chanson.
13 January 1956: live solo version with English introduction, Carnegie Hall, New York.
Accompaniment: Robert Chauvigny & His Orchestra.
To fully understand the message imparted by the song, one

has to watch the sequence in the film: the fact that Christine (Piaf) has dreamt that she has gone to heaven, leaving her penniless friends (Les Compagnons) to fend for themselves down below. Thus, as Christine is able to "return to life" assisted by Love (The Boss of Heaven, aka Marcel Vallée), the same happens to the woman who has drowned herself in the song.

There was a woman who lived without being happy. Her lover didn't love her. Funny, but that's how it was. She ran to the fountain to drown her sorrow in it. And the devil and all his followers pushed her all the way there. That's why love wept alone—why heaven understood nothing. The days of light, the words of the prayers escorted her procession. The girl died crying, *"Forgive me!"* All the flowers faded and night covered the earth, singing of the last day of this woman who died for love. Fugitives from the dark side, the unloved in a cortege set off to try and prevent the sun from rising. That's why love had no more friends, why heaven went looking for a place to shelter. The games, the dances, all the joys of the world wanted to go away. And the rotted hearts of men were going to wither away. But here, my story is going to dance under garlands of light. This couldn't last—love fixed things! And since she [the dead girl brought back to life] is singing, it's too bad for him [her lover] who's tormenting himself! *He* can cry all the time—but singing makes *her* stronger! That's why we hear the accordions—why the street bursts out in song! In all this racket we don't hear the grieving souls any more. Love's throwing a party and everyone has their heart's desire.

25: *Les yeux de ma mère* (My mother's eyes) (Edith Piaf, Robert Chauvigny).
Columbia: DFX 247 B-side of *C'est pour ca.*
Written by Piaf for Les Compagnons de la Chanson, this tells the story of the adventurer who cannot decide with whom he is the most infatuated—his mother, or his sweetheart, who may or may not be one and the same.

He was so very tall that at times you thought he'd touch the sky. He wasn't looking at you, but he was dreaming. He wasn't speaking, but he was singing: something to do with the sun. One day, he looked at the water—got on the water in search of adventure. The boys saw him dreaming, heard him singing, his eyes looking up at nature. Oh, the tender song that the boy sang! "*My mother's eyes—my sweetheart's eyes! My mother's voice—my sweetheart's voice! My mother's hands—my sweetheart's hands! For me, they're more important than life itself!*" The boat left the port. It turned its back on the North, cut through the Pacific waters: Liverpool, Panama, Santiago, Tahiti, Cuba. If it stopped in every port, he was never able to find gold. His pocket remained empty [*resta sans fortune*], while on the other hand the memories piled up, making him worry in the moonlight. And the song always followed the boy. *"My mother's eyes—my sweetheart's eyes...more important than life itself!"* But, by looking so hard we never know what we're going to find at the end of our adventures. To be honest we never knew why he fought with those hardened men. But what a fine, all-out brawl we saw there! I swear, they're still talking about it! Then the brawl ended when he was hit by a stray bullet—smack in the middle of his adventure! But the song remains that the boy sang. *"My mother's eyes—my sweetheart's eyes...more important than life itself!"*

26: *Un homme comme les autres* (A man like the others) (Edith Piaf, Pierre Roche).
8 October: Columbia DFX 246 B-side. 30cm/12-inch.
Accompaniment: Robert Chauvigny & His Orchestra.
Pierre Roche (1919-2001) was singer, pianist and composer and one half of the Aznavour-Roche duo, formed in 1944 with Charles Aznavour. The song sees Piaf reflecting on her fling with Takis Menelas.

When you think about it, a man's nothing but for the little that he interests you. He takes up space, for crying out loud! The one I have a weakness for isn't a particularly nice boy, but he resembles my song. A man like the others, among so many others! Even

47

so, nobody else has his voice, his eyes. When I see him, I'm overwhelmed. And I love him! We have our nights filled with love, crushed up against him until first light, when we make love. A man, like the others.

Their affair, however, has not endured:

It's months now, since he left. People told me that time heals. Perhaps they lied. I feel like I'm going mad! I'll never, never forget him. I'll wait for him until the very end! A man, like the others…And, closing my eyes I suddenly see him again, running his hands through my hair, and I love him! A man, like the others…and in my memories I see us dancing. I snuggle up against him, and he carries me away! And I love him—a man like the others!

27: *Mais qu'est-ce que j'ai?* (But what do I have?) (Edith Piaf, Henri Betti).
November: possible acetate or tape recording.
Written by Piaf about her relationship with and split from Yves Montand. Set to music by Henri Betti (1917-2005) whose many hit songs include *C'est si bon!* There were two sets of lyrics. The one presented to Montand, written from her perspective (that the current man in her life had eyes for her alone) highlights the fact that he was using her to ascend the music-hall ladder while seeing two male lovers behind her back making it obvious that she loved him more

48

than he ever loved her. The version which Piaf performed is marked [[...]]. Harold Rome, who later supplied Piaf with an English adaptation of *Je n'en connais pas la fin*, wrote an English lyric to this one in 1949, when it was recorded by Madelyn Russell as *What Can I Do?*

But what do I have for loving her so much, that makes me want to shout from the rooftops, "*She's mine!*" I'd look silly if I did this. You'd tell me it wasn't normal, that it's crazy to love someone like that! I know, but there you are. I can't help myself!

[[But what do I have for loving him so much that makes me want to sing from the rooftops—that he's mine, and mine alone? I've so many dreams to recall, but nobody wants to listen to me. So I start singing, and nobody can stop me anymore!]]

And when it takes over, there's nothing to be done! I love her so much, it's wonderful! I'm no longer in this world when I dream about her azure eyes, about her pure blonde hair. But what do I have, for loving her so much? A great love is wonderful when it's based on forever! There's no sadness in my heart— and it takes nothing to make me happy! Love is truly extraordinary. My feet are no longer on the ground! All my pals are making fun of me—for so far as I can see, this is the real thing! "*She's got this, she's got that! He's got this, he's got that! He's not seeing things very well! She's not seeing things very well!"* These idiots understand nothing! But, what do I have?

Piaf's visit to the United States would prove the biggest challenge of her career this far. On 30 October, she opened in a seven-week season at the Playhouse on 48th Street but if audiences were expecting another Joséphine Baker or Mistinguett bedecked in jewels and performing songs like *J'ai deux amours* and *Mon homme*, they were disappointed. What they got was this dowdy little woman clad in black, singing about lost love, prostitutes, suicide and death in a language they could not understand. Initially, Piaf hired an MC who explained what each song was about, but this robbed her performances of their continuity and he was soon dropped. Then salvation came courtesy of the distinguished theatre critic, Virgil Thompson, who devoted an entire column to her on the front page of the *Herald Tribune* which concluded:

> Her power of dramatic projection is tremendous. She is a great artiste because she gives you a clear vision of the scene or subject she is depicting, with a minimum injection of personality. Such a concentration at once of professional authority and of personal modesty is no end impressive.

And where the American public was concerned, Piaf would never look back.

Marianne Michel

Takis Menelas

With Marcel Vallee in *Neuf garçons, une fille*.

The Decca Recordings

1947

Prior to signing her Columbia contract at the end of 1945, Piaf's manager, Louis Barrier, had entered into negotiations with Decca, when the company's executives had agreed to a temporary contract comprising ten songs. The date for the sessions had been so long in coming that Barrier had assumed they would never take place, which was why the live recordings of these songs had been assigned to the Columbia vaults for future release—they would eventually be released posthumously. Now, Piaf found herself legally bound to record these ten songs, but as her Columbia contract stipulated that she could only record for *this* company in France, the Decca sessions took place at their Fonior-SA-Studio in Brussels, where artistes as diverse as Charles Trenet and the Rolling Stones would subsequently record.

28: *Le geste* (The gesture) (Michel Émer).
7 February: Decca MB 8180 A-side.
Accompaniment: Raymond Legrand & His Orchestra.
Piano: Robert Chauvigny.
Raymond Legrand (1908-74) was the father of Michel, and one of his three wives was the singer Colette Renard.

> Often enough, misfortune knocks on the door.
> That's fate, hounding us! Each new day brings new

torments that drive us even more crazy. It's there, lurking. It grabs us, holds us, captures us. Above all, we must keep a cool head (*ne pas perdre la tête*) and quietly tell ourselves, "*It'll pass, like everything else! Don't worry about it! Just make a little gesture! The good times will return! Let's forget about our woes! Everything will work out!*" He was a man with big, sad, gloomy eyes. He adored me, I was crazy about him. But he was jealous—even his own shadow rendered him crazy when night fell. He was afraid I'd grow weary of him, someday—that I'd leave with another lover. So, to make his great sadness go away I gently told him, "*It'll pass, like everything else! Don't worry about it! Just make a little gesture! Afterwards, you won't think about it anymore! Take me in your arms—you'll forget your woes! Everything will work out!*" We loved each other like they do in poems, and spent all our time telling each other, "*I'll love you forever, dear, and our dreams will be endless!*"

And of course, her story has an unhappy ending, though in this instance she is optimistic about the future:

He left, taking away all my dreams. I've nothing—neither his eyes, nor his arms. I'm left only with thoughts that one dies for. So I murmur to myself, "*Don't worry about it! I only have to make a little gesture! Afterwards, I won't think about it anymore!*

54

Perhaps another man will come along! I'll forget all my woes! Everything will work out!"

29: *Monsieur Ernest a réussi* (Monsieur Ernest has done well for himself) (Michel Émer).
7 February: Decca MB 8180 B-side.
Accompaniment: Raymond Legrand & His Orchestra.
Piano: Robert Chauvigny.
Previous recordings released posthumously by Columbia:
31 May 1946: * tape recording Radio Suisse-Romande.
4 June 1946: * tape recording for the radio show *Neuf garçons et une fille chantaient.*
* Accompaniment: Robert Chauvigny & His Orchestra.
Another of those strange lyrics where Piaf flits between tenses, seemingly for no reason.

I'm cloakroom attendant at the *Lion d'Or* and at *l'Écu d'France*. Monsieur Ernest comes here often, and each time makes advances. He squeezed me hard. He spoke of "*heart*" and "*chaumière*" [here, the term can mean "country cottage", alternatively "wagging tongues"], and finally one day I accepted. Monsieur Ernest had done well to get me to leave my cloakroom. We left on a party night. He so turned my head that we stayed together all night long. Since then, I've lived with him in his little seventh-floor room. We don't have a cent, but I love him. Monsieur Ernest has done well for himself. He's stubborn, pushy—gets what he wants!

Nothing's beyond him, I must say. He wagered that within a year he'd be a millionaire, at least. Now, he's earning so much money that he doesn't know what to do with it. Monsieur Ernest's done well for himself! Now, he does so much business that he needs three secretaries. He deals with every country from his place on rue de Passy. He works so hard that he overtires himself. He comes to see me once a week. He told me the other day, *"I've found a wealthy heiress. Naturally, it's not love, but it goes well with my career. Here, take a little money. It'll tide you over. And if you find another lover, I'll only have myself to blame!"* Monsieur Ernest's done well for himself. His career's unaffected, and I ended up back in my cloakroom. There's nothing I can do—that's life! He came here the other evening. He even had his lady with him…

Then, after the brief musical interlude she sarcastically concludes of her millionaire's stingy reward:

I was afraid there'd be a scene, but he gave me a hundred cents tip. Monsieur Ernest's *really* done well for himself!

30: *Si tu partais* (If you left) (Michel Émer).
4 February: Decca MB 8181 A-side.
Accompaniment: Raymond Legrand & His Orchestra.
Piano: Robert Chauvigny.

16 March 1947: tape recording, Radio Suisse-Romande, released posthumously.
Accompaniment: Robert Chauvigny, Marc Bonel, Marc Heyran.
Written in memory of Takis Menelas, when Piaf recalled to Michel Émer how he had pleaded with her to stay with him in Greece. In 1957/8, while touring the United States, she occasionally sang the English version, *If You Go*, with lyrics by Geoffrey Parsons. This had been first recorded by Vera Lynn in 1952, though Piaf's preferred and sanctioned version was by Peggy Lee (1961).

Our love is wonderful. Our love pleases God. It's purer, clearer than the limpid waters of the rivers. My heart suffocates when you're there. Don't spoil [*ne touche pas*] all of that! If one day you broke off our love—if one day you left for good, everything would sink into the night. The birds would no longer sing their distraught songs in their nests…the flowers would lose their scent, and that would be the end of all joy. Stay with me! Believe me, it's true that I would die if you left! For me, your eyes are more beautiful than moonlight on water. When you leave for a few minutes it's like snow in spring. You come back, you hold out your arms to me. Don't spoil that! If one day you broke off our love, if one day you left for good…I would die, if you left!

31: *Les cloches sonnent* (The bells are ringing) (Edith Piaf, Marguerite Monnot).

7 February: Decca MB 8181 B-side.

Accompaniment: Raymond Legrand & His Orchestra. Piano: Robert Chauvigny.

In this maudlin piece, Piaf sings of the behaviour of her dead neighbour's pretend friends at his wake, while telling her former lover how *she* will not be a hypocrite when *he* dies, because she has not forgiven him for treating her badly and leaving her!

> The bells are ringing this morning for the death of our neighbour. His wife's very sorrowful, but it doesn't matter to me. The people around his body, themselves close to death, pretend to be sorrowful, but I know that it doesn't matter to them. Go away, hypocrites! Death's a fantastic thing. Leave that woman to her sorrow, since it doesn't matter to you.

She then addresses her former lover:

> Do you remember, my beloved, the day you left me? People didn't give a fuck, while I myself was very sorrowful. I cast my friends aside to be alone with my body, to remember your kisses. If you'd known how much I cried! Everyone kept on laughing, and I was delirious. If you'd known how much *that* made me cry! One day, the bells will ring full blast—and it will be for you, my beloved. Your

final hour will have come. Your friends will be around you. They'll all say, *"This poor friend was an amazing boy!"* And while not giving a fuck I can already hear the bells ringing for the death of my beloved, who made me cry so, so much—like they're ringing this morning for the death of our neighbour. Ring, bells, ring, since it doesn't matter to me anymore!

32: *Sophie* (Edith Piaf, Norbert Glanzberg).
7 February: Decca OMB 15 002, A-side, 30cm/12-inch.
March: soundstage recording for the film, *Neuf garçons, un coeur*.
Accompaniment: Raymond Legrand & His Orchestra.
Piano: Robert Chauvigny.
As with *C'est pour ça*, to comprehend the context of the song one needs to watch the segment of the film where, in heaven, Christine (Piaf) is invited to the stage to sing about the suicide of a friend to an audience of "dead" people who are now angels, and who disappear when the song ends.

> When you were alive, you called yourself Sophie, and you were beautiful. Mademoiselle Sophie! Your dreams filled with madness made you the loveliest! You had beautiful hair, a delicious smile, your eyes filled with dreams. What a wonderful human being you were, when alive!

And then, she explains how Sophie's bubble was burst:

A man without imagination, one you fancied, entered your life. He told you, *"Darling, I'll love you forever!"* He lied to you….Living only for him, you let all your friends go. But he didn't understand. One day, he left. Oh, Mademoiselle Sophie! Goodbye, fantasy! Goodbye, madness! You no longer loved life. One sad rainy evening gave God the desire to take your life….But what possessed you to leave us like that, without telling us anything? You killed life. You're in heaven, Mademoiselle Sophie!

33: *Une chanson à trois temps* (A song in triple-time) (Anna Marly).
10 February: Decca OMB 15 002 B-side, 30cm/12-inch.
Accompaniment: Raymond Legrand & His Orchestra.
Previous recordings, released posthumously by Columbia:
4 June 1946: * tape recording for the radio show *Neuf garçons et une fille chantaient*.
Accompaniment: Robert Chauvigny & His Orchestra.
16 March 1947: tape recording, Radio Suisse-Romande.
Opens with the introduction to *Sous les ponts de Paris*.
Accompaniment: Robert Chauvigny, Marc Bonel, Marc Heyran.
Anna Marly (1917-2006) was a Russian-born French singer –songwriter best-known for *Le chant des Partisans*, the unofficial anthem of the Free French during World War II. The lyric, about a man who picks up prostitutes and leaves them to die, incarcerated, also alludes to Marly's confessed

non-comprehension of some French songs—while itself not always making a great deal of sense in parts. The term *une chanson à trois temps* refers to the typical French song comprising three verses and three refrains.

> Nothing to ask of you anymore. Let each one keep their problems. What does it matter if it's going to snow, if it's going to rain? There are no more knights [i.e., in shining armour]. Each for his own, and the same goes for you, the street singer, singing on the pavement for those who are in love. Off she goes, humming a song in triple-time that doesn't rhyme at all—but which charms the stranger who doesn't give a damn! And tomorrow, everyone will be singing it in the street without knowing what it's about, or bothering to find out. A song in triple-time that drives you up the wall [*qui traverse les murs*] It's a love-story of a dumb blonde [une Suzon] or a tough-guy. But you forget the story—it's the melody you retain—the song in triple-time. This is Parisian!

Then she realises that she remembers the story, after all:

> It was a day like so many others. A stranger came to Paris. She'd believed the yarn he'd spun to her [rough translation: *elle avait cru au bel apôtre*] about the easy joys of life. He installed her in a grey, ruined palace next to the river and, leaving her his new cape, left her there for the rest of her life. So she's now dragging out her sadness in triple-time more painful than anything, affirming that there are

61

people who don't give a damn about springtime, about birds, about girls who believe in everything! A sadness in triple-time that rhymes with so much that she'll die of it, in a year or three! But nobody around her will notice, for the story is forgotten and only the melody remains. A sadness in triple-time. This is Parisian!

And, the inevitable tragic ending to the story:

> She died of it, as the others die—in her palace, one windy evening. They buried her among the others in the Innocents' Cemetery, where each Saturday visitors amuse themselves reading the stones and daydream songs in triple-time. Was her pathway through life much tormented? Therefore is it too much trouble for you passers-by to stop and pray for her. We may stand tall, but we'll end up as dust. And do we have to be romantic poets [*poètes d'amour*] to leave songs behind that last? For it's the story that we forget, and the melody that we retain. A love affair in triple-time. This is Parisian!

At this point, Piaf had recorded six of the ten songs for Decca, but refused to commit to any more for this year, citing her heavy work schedule. Her manager Louis Barrier had booked her on a lengthy provincial tour, along with her next recording session for Columbia in the early summer. A compromise was reached wherein she would fulfil the rest of her contract in the autumn—but this was put off until the following year when Barrier announced that he had booked Piaf to appear in New York.

February 1947: at the Fonior-SA-Studio in Brussels
Recording *Monsieur Ernest a reussi.*

1948

An 18-months hiatus separated Piaf's recording sessions with Decca—taken up by touring France and the United States, and studio sessions with Columbia. Even so, she was reluctant to complete her commitment to the company, and after the first session in June when just one song was recorded, declared that she would not be returning to Brussels to put down the remaining songs—until the Decca executives threatened legal action.

The Aznavour-Roche duo had accompanied Piaf to New York as part of the package which had also included Michel Émer, on "standby" for emergency songs. It was Aznavour (1924-2018) who coined the term 'Piaf's Boys' for her lovers: once each man had been thus recognized, he would be supplied with his "uniform and accoutrements": blue serge suit and matching navy blue tie, a car—more than one, if he could not make up his mind which colour he preferred—gold cufflinks, tie-pin and cigarette lighter. And if the lover was truly special, the lighter would be platinum.

Upon learning that Aznavour wrote his own material, Piaf asked him to write her a song, leaving him to choose the theme. With his partner, Pierre Roche, he presented her with a maudlin piece which was recorded during her first Decca session. Then, just days after this session and for reasons which were never explained—least of all to Aznavour himself—the company announced that it had been archived, and that Piaf would have to return to the studio and record a replacement.

34: *Il pleut* (1) (It's raining) (Charles Aznavour, Pierre Roche).
15 June: acetate, never released.
Accompaniment: Raymond Legrand & His Orchestra.
Piano: Robert Chauvigny.

It's raining. The brollies [umbrellas], sad friends, emerge one by one like huge mushrooms from the houses. It's raining. The whole town is wet. The houses have caught a cold. The gutters have snotty noses. It's raining, as if by order. The birds are deserting the sky. Clouds and wolves [Aznavour's way of saying that it was raining cats and dogs]! The windows have tears in their eyes. Fine days all seem to be in mourning, and we hear the pitter-patter. The town has no more harmony. Alone, the streets are bored. It's raining. I hear it when it's dripping. The rain disgusts me—on the roads, all around me. The drips don't give a fuck! Doubtless they don't know that my heart's lost its love and is in disarray! It's raining...Nature's loaded with boredom. High above, everything's dressed in grey. Heaven's sulking! My nose pressed against the window-pane, I let the tears flow. It's raining within my heart of lost dreams. It's raining on my love and my endless sorrows, just like it is in the street.

Piaf re-recorded *Il pleut* for Columbia in July, and this time *she* requested that the recording be archived, in the wake of a furious row that had taken place with Aznavour, a few days after the session, as he explained:

> I presented her *Je hais les dimanches*. "It's shit," she said. "Give it to Juliette Gréco or Lucienne Delyle. That way they'll have a song of their own and stop stealing mine." So I did this, and Piaf went crazy. It took her two more years to forgive me, though I kept on working with her, and eventually she began singing my songs.

Piaf would never like Juliette Gréco, and always pretended not to like Lucienne Delyle, though she would eventually write a song especially for her. In the meantime, she returned to the Decca studios in Brussels.

35: *Monsieur X* (Roger Goze, Michel Émer)
12 July: Decca MB 20 242, B-side.
Accompaniment: Raymond Legrand & His Orchestra.

> I got to know him, somewhere or other. That's not important, likewise the time. I didn't know his age. Was he right in the head? It would be wise of me to keep quiet about his name. He walks along the streets from La Villette to l'Opéra—here are the banks of the Seine. He meets people. "*Hello—how are you?*" He goes without difficulty along the streets—without difficulty, but certainly without joy

66

from the Bastille to the Madeleine to queue for the cinema. His noble title is his only possession. Surely he must have done his bit during his youth [*son devoir*, referring to military service]? At his place, in a glass case are medals. He must have gone to war—it's [the glass case] filled with citations. He walks along the streets…since the evening when his wife followed a handsome lad just like a dog. He did nothing to get her to come back, and perhaps it's best this way.

And of course, the tragic but somewhat confusing end to the mystery man's story, where we are left wondering why his funeral cortege ends up outside the cinema!

The cold, and not caring less, got the better of him. He died without suffering—his concierge told us. Life was too hard, the machine worn out. A car [the hearse] rolled through the streets taking him to La Villette and l'Opéra…People made the sign of the Cross. From the Bastille to the Madeleine, it stands in line at the cinema.

36: *Les vieux bateaux* (The old boats) (Jacques Bourgeat, Jacqueline Batell)
12 July 1948: Decca MB 20 242, A-side.
Accompaniment: Raymond Legrand & His Orchestra.
Jacqueline Batell was Suzy Solidor's pianist. Jacques Bourgeat (1888-1966) was a poet and man of letters—and a

close friend of Piaf's whom she had met at Gerny's in 1935, and who would remain one of her confidants for the rest of her life. In this poem, the old ships themselves are telling their story, alternating between rambling and reminiscing. The naval commanders referred to are Jean Bart (1650-1702) and Robert Surcouf (1773-1827).

The ones who once sailed around the world, with dovetail grace from the Loire to Guadalquivir, have only their memories. In the basin where their masts resemble treetops, they meditate on their past which made them widowers of adventures. One was a schooner back then—the other an Empire frigate. He was only a little ship when he was fighting the English. And now, they're little more than old, floating wrecks whose heads ramble on about exploits gone by. "*I saw the plague in Singapore in 1777,*" says one fat-bellied ancestor. "*I was the love of Monsieur Vigny, you know—the poet and aristocrat!*" "'*How beautiful my frigate was* [he said]*!'—Well, he was talking about me!*" "*You seem to set me apart* [from the others]*! It's true, my hull's marked 'RAGE'!*" "*I can confer—it read* COURAGE!*" "*I served under Jean Bart, before his second godfather. It was a good war. A cannonball from England gave me the notch I wear in my groin!*" "*My commander was Surcouf. Shining in his fist and dripping with blood was a gouged-out eye! Brown bodies fell—without saying 'Ouf!'*" "*My* *name was 'Bellérophon'. I saw him, dreaming beneath my foresail before he went to St Helena—a man named Napoleon!"* And thus, rocked by the lapping of the sheltering docks, their souls scattered, the old boats chat to one another about their past—happy in their serenity, telling stories about old sailors. And in the distance, some small rowing-boat shouts, *"Grub up!"*

Piaf's final—and reluctant—visit to the Fonior-SA-Studio was to record two songs. The first was a more optimistic replacement for *Il pleut*. Jacques Larue and Piaf's former orchestra leader Wal-Berg had written *Amour du mois de mai* in 1943 for the film *Après l'orage* (After The Storm), when it had been performed by Claude Robin. Renée Lebas (1917-2009), a popular singer of the day with whom Piaf frequently clashed, had recently revived it and it had been added to the soundtrack of *Scandale aux Champs-Élysées*, along with *Boléro*, which Piaf later sang, and *Mademoiselle de Paris*.

37: *Amour du mois de mai* (Maytime love) (Wal-Berg, Jacques Larue).
6 August 1948: Decca MEI 20 260, A-side.
Accompaniment: Raymond Legrand & His Orchestra.

Maytime love! You smell the joy, light as a cornflower! You bloom in our hearts! Lovers dance in the meadows, on the quaysides. Flowers make up bouquets…My love, swear to me that we'll love each other for ever! My love—what a beautiful day for my heart! The accordion's squeezing out a song. A boy's getting close to a see-through bodice—since they love each other forever, he's no need to be afraid! Your eyes are two cornflowers that I hold in my heart. My love, you know only too well that we'll always love each other! Maytime love! You smell the joy…you bloom in our hearts, but the most beautiful love is like a sweet refrain. We know some of the words, but forget how it ends. My love! Another perhaps will say to your heart, "*My love!*"

38: *Cousu du fil blanc* (It's obvious) (Michel Émer).
6 August 1948: Decca MEI 20 260, B-side.
Accompaniment: Raymond Legrand & His Orchestra.
Cousu de fil blanc translates literally as "sewn with white thread", meaning that if a dark garment is stitched up with white cotton, the stitching is pronounced. The term equates to English expressions such as "blatantly obvious", "plain as the nose on your face", etc.

It was one spring evening. I was twenty—walking, laughing and singing when I saw his very blue eyes as he passed by. He approached me and murmured in his warm voice, "*I don't think it's the first time that we've seen each other!*" It was obvious! He was wrong, searching for complicated words. All he

70

had to do to make me fall in love with him was talk. It was obvious! He saw only too well that I was lying when I told him, *"I can only stay for a moment—someone's waiting for me!"* It was blatantly obvious when he squeezed my hand and I told him, *"That's not good!"* And yet I left him…

The lovers then move to the next stage in their relationship:

How he caressed me well! We didn't say anything to each other—we simply made love. Our love was wonderful. It seemed that the gods were only thinking about the two of us. We were so happy, and we wanted our nights to last a lifetime. Our hearts cried out as one [*n'avaient qu'un cri*]: *"My love, my darling! I love you too much!"*

And then, the inevitable rupture:

It was blatantly obvious! He left, one morning. I thought I was going to die of grief. I cursed Fate for bringing us together [rough translation: *qui m'avait mise sur son chemin*]. It was blatantly obvious, like that spring morning when I was twenty—walking, laughing and singing, when I saw this marvellous tall boy passing by. He knew only too well that I was lying. *"I can only stay for a moment!"* He squeezed my hand, and I only saw his blue eyes. Yet we didn't say anything to each other. We simply made love. It was blatantly…heaven!

The Playhouse

FIRE NOTICE: The exit indicated by a red light and sign nearest to the seat you occupy is the shortest route to the street. In the event of fire please do not run—WALK TO THAT EXIT.

Frank J. Quayle
FIRE COMMISSIONER

Thoughtless persons annoy patrons and distract actors and endanger the safety of others by lighting matches during the performance and intermissions. This violates a city ordinance and renders the offender liable to a summons from the fireman on duty. It is urged that all patrons refrain from lighting matches in the auditorium of this theatre.

THE PLAYBILL A WEEKLY PUBLICATION OF PLAYBILL INCORPORATED

Beginning Thursday, October 30, 1947   *   Matinees Saturday and Sunday

CLIFFORD C. FISCHER

presents

EDITH PIAF

and

Her Continental Entertainers

including

LES COMPAGNONS DE LA CHANSON

and

GEORGES ANDRE MARTIN, Conferencier

GEORGE AND TIM DORMONDE   LES CANOVA

LYDA ALMA AND VANNI FLEURY   WINTER SISTERS

Dorritt Merrill, Announcer

The playbill for Piaf's New York debut.

Columbia: Period Two ~ Part 1

1948

Piaf and the boxer Marcel Cerdan (1916-49) had first met at the Club des Cinq, in Paris, in December 1946. Known as "The Moroccan Bomber", he was a stocky, unattractive man of average height, with a mouthful of gold fillings and a tough face which, at the time, she said had given him the "lived-in" look. No one will ever be able to explain why she fell in love with him. He was the only one of her lovers who was her professional equal. He did not come from her musical side of the fence, therefore had nothing to offer her other than himself. She could do nothing to further enhance his career, and he remained the greatest love of her life *solely* because he died while they were at the zenith of their affair—not giving her the opportunity to dispense with him once he had served his purpose or she had tired of him, as happened with every one of the others.

Piaf and Cerdan met again at a cocktail party in New York in December 1947—one of the guests was Marlene Dietrich, who became a lifelong friend, and recalled:

> Everyone thought Piaf was a fragile little bird, but such a thing could not have been further from the truth—though she wasn't at all like that horrible caricature in the play [Pam Gems' *Piaf*]. She and I spent a lot of time together at the beginning of 1948. I'd finished making *Foreign Affair* and a film

I don't even care to remember [*Jigsaw*], so I had all the time in the world to help her with her American career. One of our first conversations was about *La vie en rose*, when she complained about that singer who'd sung it before her [Marlene was referring not to Marianne Michel, but Charles Trenet's lover, Roland Gerbeau]. Edith couldn't stand the man. She told me, 'Every time I heard him singing my song on the radio, I wanted to rush out of the room and throw up. I started wishing that I'd never written the fucking thing.' And then, she met Cerdan…

Cerdan was in New York training for a fight, and his team did everything they could to keep him away from Piaf and avoid a scandal—he was married, with three children. For the time being, their machinations appeared to be working. In the spring of 1948, Piaf returned to Paris, where she opened in a season at the ABC. On Sunday 16 May, she gave a "command performance" at Chez Carrere, just off the Champs-Elysées, for the six-months-wed Princess Elizabeth and Prince Philip. The couple were on their first official visit to Paris, Elizabeth was pregnant (though the news was yet to be announced), and Piaf was asked to sing "something pleasant as befitted a cultured young royal". Her programme included *La vie en rose* and the yet-to-be-recorded *Les feuilles mortes* and *Pleure pas*, but this was it so far as "light-hearted" songs were concerned, and she went on to perform new songs currently being tested with audiences before being committed to shellac: *Le ciel est fermé* tells of the fate which will befall Man should God go on strike; *Tous les amoureux chantent* tells of the lovers mown down by a car while dancing in the street. And *Monsieur Lenoble*—of which Michel Émer recalled:

> I remember the first time I went to America with her. I was looking forward to having a night on the town with the rest of the gang and seeing the sights of New York—but she confined me to my room, locking the door from the outside, saying that she would only let me out after I'd written her a song. I did better than that, and wrote two. *Bal dans ma rue* is about a woman who introduces her lover to her best friend—who subsequently runs off with him. And *Monsieur Lenoble* told of the man who takes everyone for granted, most especially his wife who leaves him for a younger man. Piaf was always looking for a new way to die, and in this one he gasses himself. The Americans used to howl with laughter when she imitated the hissing of the gas-taps.

39: *Monsieur Lenoble* (Michel Émer).
12 June: Columbia BF 189, B-side (as *T'as pas profité de ta chance*). *
August: Columbia DF 3244, B-side (as *Monsieur Lenoble*), reissue. *
December: live performance, Copacabana, Paris. Released posthumously. **

2 June 1955: live recording, Porte Saint-Jean, Québec, released posthumously. *

4 January 1956: live version, with English introduction. Carnegie Hall, New York. *

Accompaniment: * Robert Chauvigny & His Orchestra.
** Daniel White & His Orchestra.

American audiences assumed this was a comic song and laughed on account of Piaf exchanging the phrase "*T'as pas profité de ta chance!*" (You didn't take advantage of your good luck!) for "*You missed the bus, honey!*"

> Monsieur Lenoble is very sad since his wife left him for a very young artist she got to know this summer. He listens to the melody she loved. Bit by bit, those few notes poison him forever.

Piaf repeats what the music is telling him, inside his head:

> *You didn't take advantage of your good luck, my friend! You were too sure of yourself (Tu avais trop de confiance)! It's over. You had a wonderful wife! So lovely! You didn't know how to make her happy! You're all alone—she left!*

And then:

> Monsieur Lenoble tries to see reason. He thinks about all that he's done. His intentions were good, though he wasn't perfect...Perhaps he didn't have a

very good character. He got angry over nothing, but at the office his colleagues thought him a good man.

And after hearing the voice once more inside his head, there is but one solution for his anguish:

Monsieur Lenoble blows his nose, puts on his nightshirt, switches on the gas and gets into bed. Tomorrow, it will all be over. And Monsieur Lenoble thinks about the one he adored.

And now, the gas-tap speaks to him inside his head:

You didn't take advantage of your good luck, my friend! You were too sure of yourself...

The song ends with Piaf dramatically elongating the final syllable of the word *confiance* as a way of emulating the hissing of the gas tap.

40: *Les amants de Paris* (The lovers of Paris) (Eddy Marnay, Léo Ferré).
12 June: Columbia BF 189, A-side.
August: Columbia DF 3244, A-side, reissue. See **#39**.
4 January 1956: live solo version, with English introduction. Carnegie Hall, New York.
Accompaniment: Robert Chauvigny & His Orchestra.
Choir: Raymond Saint-Paul.
Léo Ferré (1916-93) was a French singer-songwriter famed

more for his anarchic interpretations than for this lyrically confusing one. Chez Robinson was the famous Parisian tree-house dance hall and restaurant.

The lovers of Paris are making love to my song. In Paris lovers make love any way that suits them. The refrains I tell them are more beautiful than sunny days. They make lots of springtimes, and springtime creates love! My verse got lost around the edge of a garden. It was never given back to me, so I'm well aware that the lovers of Paris stole my songs! In Paris, lovers have strange ways! The lovers of Paris make their way to Robinson, where hits end up played on the accordion. The lovers of Paris are about to enter a new season, dragging my little bit of a song by the hand. There's gold a-plenty and lots of lilacs for them to see. That's how love affairs usually start...I hold the chains of love in both hands. There are millions of lovers, and I only have one tune. All around us we see boys from all over the world who would give up springtime to have a go at love. And springtime's not such a great price to pay, since I plastered the warm month of May all over their calendars! The lovers of Paris have worn out my songs. In Paris, lovers make love any way that it suits them. Give us some songs, so that we can make love to each other in Paris!

41: *Boléro* (Henri Contet, Paul Durand)
July: possible acetate.
Piaf performed this on stage, and Lucienne Delyle released a cover version which was a big hit. Mitchell Parish wrote an English-language version, *All My Love*, which Piaf performed in America, and whose lyrics have nothing to do with the originals. This was introduced to the British public by Gracie Fields in Britain—while Patti Page's recording topped the US charts in 1950, her first Number 1.

> Bolero, in the sweetness of evening, under the red and black sky where the guitars are playing! Bolero—if you want to dance in my tight embrace! It would be good to make love! Come, my love—I'm calling you to come and dance again! Bolero—I'll always remember the day when I danced with love! As in a dream, the rising night ignites a flame. Deep within our souls, the sunshine of your eyes—a wonderful moment! So that I can take your hand in mine, tell me words of hope while you're dancing. Tell me your desire! Bolero—like a first sigh in the sweetness of evening, under the black and red sky!

42: *Pot pourri: Le petit homme/ Je m'en fous pas mal/ Un refrain courait dans la rue/ Qu'as tu fait, John?*
July: Columbia DFX 248 A-side 30 cm/12-inch.
Accompaniment: Guy Luypaerts & His Orchestra, Marius Coste & His Orchestra.

43: *J'entends* (I'm listening) (Tom Waltham, Louis Sauvat).

July: possible tape recording or acetate.

Tom Waltham (1897-1974) was a British bandleader and jazz pianist, popular in France at the time. There were two versions: the French one, with lyrics by Louis Sauvat, and an English adaptation, *Criminal*, by Ralph Hedges which Piaf may have performed in New York at the Versailles. It is possible that either or both may have been recorded—the songs were registered with Éditions Masspacher and the sheet-music printed. If so, they have yet to surface.

44: *La valse de la bonne humeur* (The good-humoured waltz) (Maurice Martelier, Eldo di Lazzaro).

July: possible tape recording or acetate.

This song, not at all in keeping with the typical Piaf repertoire, is listed in the archives of Éditions Musicali di Lazzaro-Milano as having been recorded by her, but as yet has not surfaced. It was recorded by The Jacques Hélian Orchestra, with the comedian Zappy Max on vocals. Eldo di Lazzaro (1902-68) was an Italian songwriter whose most famous work was *Reginella campagnola*, adapted into English as *The Woodpecker Song*.

> We're singing the good-humoured waltz. Tra-la-la! Put your heart into it, like me! Take a deep breath. Let the storm pass quietly. Life's so beautiful, no need to worry. My melody will make you forget everything. We're singing the good-humoured waltz

and your worries will just go away when singing this charming little tune. There are mixed-up people—obsessed, despairing about everything. They'd search a hundred leagues for the happiness that God gives us on earth. Get rid of that dejected attitude and petty miseries. Believe me, the best way to be as happy as kings is to do what I'm doing! We're singing the good-humoured waltz. Tra-la-la! Take a cream coffee to bed with you, and cakes and hot croissants! We're singing the good-humoured waltz. She's [the song does not specify whom] selling post cards and pencils because she was fated to sell pencils. It's stupid, eh?

45: *Il pleut* (Version 2) (It's raining) Charles Aznavour, Pierre Roche).
19 July: Columbia DF 3283, B-side.
Accompaniment: Robert Chauvigny.
The lyrics are the same as Item **#34** recorded for Decca.

46: *Leyiz M'Plorer/ Gilles a perdu* (Let me weep/Gilles has lost) (Nicolas Defrecheux, Monpou).
July: tape recording, possibly Radio Suisse-Romande, released posthumously.
Piano accompaniment: Robert Chauvigny.
A curiosity, penned in 1854 by the Belgian poet Nicolas Defrecheux (1825-74). Here, Piaf assumes the identity of the recently-bereaved Gilles. She reads the poem in French so that her listeners will understand what it is about, before

singing it in its original Liége-Wallon dialect with Les Compagnons de la Chanson.

My comrades came to tell me, *"There's a party today. Come along!"* Let the others have fun. I'm weeping for my mistress, who has left me. I loved her so much, and she's in my thoughts, day and night. Let me weep, my friends. My life's a mess. I've lost her. Her small white hands had the same pallor as our lilies, and her sweet lips were pinker than our rose bush. And no one knew how to sing love songs like her. Let me weep, my friends...You would have thought an angel had stopped by on earth. She was so good—to her friends, to those who were unhappy, towards orphans, towards her mother. Let me weep, my friends...I may never see the season of violets again because she told me, *"Look at those flowers, and the birds that are singing! Doesn't it sound like a day for celebration? When we love each other, every day of the year is beautiful!"* Let me weep, my friends...She's now in heaven, high above the stars. What made her leave without me? Whatever you say, I must forget her. But, can I? Let me weep, my friends. My life's a mess. I've lost her!

47: *Il a chanté* (He sang) (Cécile Didier, Marguerite Monnot).
21 July: Columbia DFX 248, B-side 30cm/12-inch.

Accompaniment: Robert Chauvigny & His Orchestra.
Duet with Fred Mella of Les Compagnons de la Chanson, who sings vocalese throughout the refrain.
Cécile Didier (1888-1975) was a stage and film actress. So far as is known, this is the only lyric she penned.

He came for the harvesting. He was a strong and handsome boy with tender eyes and hardened lips. He sang while harvesting, and within his voice we heard all of Nature's voices. He sang of the bright spring, of birds, of shining meadows, of green copses and budding flowers. In the evening, for the people who were gathered and to the stooping sheaves [*la fausse courbe des javelles*], he sang the song of the meadows. He sang. The harvesters listened to him, and the Mistress listened to him too. He sang, then he said, *"Here's to my health—and tomorrow I'll be on my way!"* Around midnight, when everyone was asleep, he was leaving without making a sound when the Mistress came—pale, her heart beating fast, beautiful, desirable, almost naked beneath her cloak. She said, *"I've waited for you for days, for years. Who cares if life is short?* [Qu'importe une existence brève?] *Stay with me until dawn. Sing me the love song so that I can finally live out my dream!"* He sang. Eyes closed, she listened to his sweet voice that took her in. He sang of love, of death, of sensual pleasure. And both of them went on their way the next day. She learned things the hard way [*Elle a connu l'âpres chemin*]. Hunger, work, sadness, for her lover quickly tired of her. With no regrets about the past, he caressed other mistresses.

And suicide—it would appear by swallowing poison—is her only way out:

> No longer able to put up with any more, after nights and days of hell, the poor woman said, "*Beloved, don't feel any remorse. Sing me the song of death, and leave me. I'm happy!*" He sang. Eyes closed, she listened. The great shudder burned her throughout. He sang. With a sigh, she passed away. Then he went on his way.

Not long after this final session, Piaf and Marcel Cerdan sailed for New York where the biggest fight of his career—the World Middleweight Championship against Tony Zale, took place on 2 September at New Jersey's Roosevelt Stadium. Cerdan won, and three weeks later Piaf opened at the Versailles, playing to packed houses until 14 December. Four days later, she and Cerdan returned to France, where he was invited to the Élysée Palace for a private audience with President Auriol—while Piaf opened in a season at the Copacabana cabaret, in Paris, the premiere of which was recorded and broadcast on French radio on 20 June 1949, and also by the BBC as part of their *Rendezvous in Paris* series.

During the run-up to the American tour and immediately afterwards, Piaf performed several songs on stage which she would not get around to recording until after her return to France, some as late as the summer of 1950. The arrangements/orchestras vary between the live recordings and those put down in the studio:

48: *You're Too Dangerous, Cheri* (Mack David, Edith Piaf, Louiguy.

December: live performance, Copacabana, Paris. Released posthumously. Never recorded in the studio.

Accompaniment: Daniel White & His Orchestra.

The first English-language version of *La vie en rose*.

Recorded in 1947 in the USA by Hal Derwin (1914-98), it also appeared on the B-side of Buddy Clark's *Pianissimo* the same year. Dinah Shore scored a hit with it the following year, when it was covered by Gracie Fields, who also recorded *Take Me To Your Heart Again*, the second English language version of *La vie en rose.*

49: *Pour moi toute seule* (For me, all alone) (Flavien Monod, Michel Philippe-Gérard, Guy Lafarge).

December: live at the Copacabana, Paris.

Accompaniment: Daniel White & His Orchestra.

9 February: Columbia BF 133, B-side.

Accompaniment: Robert Chauvigny & His Orchestra.

An English-language version of the song, *Misery in Mink (I May Be Blue)*, orchestrated close to the Piaf original, was recorded by the British actress-comedian Dora Bryan for an album in 1964. Though the subject may not be a prostitute, the sleeve-notes describe it as "a tart-inspired number, bathed in sleazy saxophones and lazy jazz-tones that lend it an instant air of scandal." Flavien Monod (1920-93) famously collaborated with Guy Lafarge (1904-90) on *La Seine*, introduced the previous year by Jacqueline François. Michel Philippe-Gérard (1924-2014) would subsequently write hits for just about every major French singer.

Faded walls, joyless days. Worn curtains, a bed that's too cold. Here and there a heart. Worries, embarrassments. Fortunately, I sleep! For me, all alone, night's just fallen…The dream has begun, and will end tomorrow morning. I know that only too well, but I'm all right. I'm speaking softly to myself. Don't disturb me! Eight o'clock, all in a dash. Dirty job, features drawn. Greasy spoon, dirty winter, dirty Métro, newspaper articles. Fortunately, I sleep! For me, all alone, night's just fallen…don't disturb me!

And for once, the song ends on an *almost* positive note:

In the warmth of my winter, a name sings in my house. Here and there a heart. No more worries and embarrassments. For me, all alone, love has just arrived…The dream has begun! What will happen when tomorrow comes? I've no idea. But I'm all right. I'm quietly loving him. Don't disturb us!

87

50: *Le prisonnier de la tour* (The prisoner in the Tower) (Gérard Calvi, Francis Blanche).

December: life performance at the Copacabana, Paris. Released posthumously.

Accompaniment: Daniel White & His Orchestra.

9 February 1949: Columbia BF 128, B-side.

Accompaniment: Robert Chauvigny & His Orchestra.

Francis Blanche (1921-74) was an actor-humourist known for his partnership with Pierre Dac (1893-1975). Gérard Calvi (1922-2015) wrote the score for three *Asterix* films. The song features a conversation between the girl and her grandmother, whose name is repeated to the point of tediousness. It begins formally (*vous*) and ends intimately (*tu*). It was performed by Les Compagnons de la Chanson in the 1951 film, *Paris chante toujours!* also featuring Piaf.

> ISABELLE: The prisoner in the Tower killed himself this morning, grandmother. We won't be attending Mass tomorrow…He flung himself off the Tower…while reaching out his hands towards me. It seems to me that I'm sorrowful.
>
> GRANDMOTHER: If the King knew that, Isabelle, you would no longer have the right to wear the lace dress.
>
> ISABELLE: The prisoner in the Tower was my only friend, grandmother. We're not going to Mass today…He was my only love, the reason I'm alive…and my youth died with him.
>
> GRANDMOTHER: If the King knew that, Isabelle,

you would no longer have the right to wear the lace dress.

ISABELLE: The prisoner in the Tower waited for me each evening, grandmother. We'll never go to Mass again. It's a sin that love and the world is so badly done by... They killed *my* lover.

GRANDMOTHER: If the King knew that, Isabelle, you would no longer have the right to wear the lace dress.

ISABELLE: The prisoner in the Tower doesn't have a shroud—nothing but a black hole in which the leaves are engulfed. But I'll go there each day to weep beneath the lime trees, and nothing, not even the King, will prevent my mourning.

GRANDMOTHER: If the King knew that, Isabelle, he would want to cry with you. For he loved a beauty who wasn't meant for a King. And the beauty, Isabelle, was me.

51: *Bal dans ma rue* (Ball in my street) (Michel Émer).
December: live performance, Copacabana, Paris. Released posthumously.
Accompaniment: Daniel White & His Orchestra.
10 February: Columbia BF 128, A-side.
Accompaniment: Robert Chauvigny & His Orchestra.
Accordion: Marc Bonel. Choir: Raymond Saint-Paul.
1951: live performance in the film short, *Holiday in Paris: 14 Juillet*, BBC Television, 28 February.
Accompaniment: Robert Chauvigny & His Orchestra.

Tonight, there's a ball in my street. Never before have I seen such gaiety, such a crowd...And in the little bistro where joy is flowing, seven musicians are perched on a trestle playing for the lovers who dance together, laughing and gazing into each other's eyes. There's a ball in my street, and everyone's a little excited, maybe because they've drunk too much...

She then reflects upon what happened, the last time there was a ball, and how the current one came about:

He was so handsome when he took me out, so much so that everyone turned to stare. I was so proud of him that I couldn't resist introducing him to my best friend. They hit it off at once [*ils se sont plus immédiatement*] and were married this morning. They made an amazing couple, and I was witness [best woman]. That's why there's a ball in my street. Never before have I seen such gaiety...

52: *My Lost Melody* [1] (Raymond Asso, Harold Rome, Marguerite Monnot.
December: live performance, Copacabana, Paris. Released posthumously. A lyrically slightly different version of the one recorded in December 1950, and not the one of July of that year.
Accompaniment: Daniel White & His Orchestra.

The first of two English adaptations of *Je n'en connais pas la fin*. The American lyricist/composer Harold Rome (1908-93) worked mostly on theatre productions, but adapted several of Piaf's songs into English.

53: *La petite Marie* (Edith Piaf, Marguerite Monnot).
December: live performance, Copacabana, Paris. Released posthumously.
Accompaniment: Daniel White & His Orchestra.
11 May 1950: Columbia BF 306, B-side.
Accompaniment: Robert Chauvigny & His Orchestra.

In this song, the woman has stormed out of the house after an argument, and when she returns, she finds her lover gone. When Piaf performed this on the stage, she addressed his photograph, and imagined that he was still there, hence the repeating of the phrase, "*Yesterday—and today!*"

> While I was crossing the avenue, I bumped into someone who spoke bluntly to me:
> "*You know Little Marie—young, and more's to the point, beautiful? Well, she died this morning!*"
> "*But how so? That's horrible!*"
> "*It's worse than that! It's unbelievable!*"
> "*Yesterday…and today!*"
> "*Well, there it is! It's over!*"
> Then I thought about us: the little rows over nothing and blown out of proportion, all in our imagination. A great love isn't a big thing—not really. It doesn't

amount to much! We separate over an argument, and pride enters the fight, so we each go our own way. Look at what can happen to you! I see her again—Little Marie. My God, how beautiful she was! There are some truly unhappy blows. She had everything to make her happy. Sure enough, she wasn't unhappy! But him who's left behind—it's horrible! What's he going to do with his days—with his nights, his years? Yesterday again...and today. Their beautiful story is over. So, I think about us, about the little incidents over nothing, things blown out of proportion. All in our imagination! How did I leave you this morning? We wanted to be clever. We separated after an argument, and played the blame-game [*on a joué à cœur qui lutte*], and off you went!

Then, hysteria takes over:

I hope nothing's happened to you! Please God, pity me! Ask anything of me, but above all, don't take him away from me! Oh, my darling—you were there. I was the only one talking, as you see! My love, take me in your arms! No—say nothing! That's it, be quiet! Remember Little Marie—the kid who *so* loved life? Well, she died this morning! As you say, it's horrible—unbelievable. Hold me tight! Darling—how good I feel, in your arms!

With Marcel Cerdan, backstage
at the Versailles, New York.

1949

On 14 and 22 January, Piaf performed at the Salle Pleyel, and such was the demand for tickets that the orchestra pit was removed to accommodate 200 extra seats. She then began working on the boxing film, *L'homme aux mains d'argile* (The Man With Clay Hands)—not as a member of the cast, but putting Marcel Cerdan through his paces as an actor, playing himself. As a matter of course she was asked to contribute to the soundtrack, with a song telling us how she misses the city of her birth when she is far away.

54: *Paris* (André Bernheim)
3 February: Columbia BF, 133 A-side.
Accompaniment: Robert Chauvigny & His Orchestra.
From the film, *L'homme aux mains d'argile*.

> We recall the songs. A wintry evening, chilled faces. Chestnut sellers, a room on the fifth-floor. Cream coffees on a morning. Montparnasse and the Café du Dôme. The suburbs and the Latin Quarter. The Tuileries and the Place Vendôme. Paris was gaiety—sweetness too, our tenderness. Paris—your kids and artisans, your peddlars and pimps, your spring mornings! Paris—the smell of your cobblestones, your chestnut trees. I think of you all the time. Paris—I miss you, old friend. We'll be together again, my great Paris! Evidently, times can get a little difficult. But, my word! Everything turns

out well—with Paris, it's so easy! For me, Paris represents fine days—tunes that are light-hearted, harsh, or tender. For me, Paris represents my loves, and my heart can't take any more! Paris *is* gaiety…and we'll be together again!

55: *Dany* (Edith Piaf, Marguerite Monnot)
3 February: DF 3283, B-side.
Accompaniment: Robert Chauvigny & His Orchestra.

In a port, there's a bar. At the counter, one sees eyes as black as evening. They call him Dany. All the women are crazy about him. When night comes, above the noise we hear the cries, *"Oh, Dany! Oh, my Dany! We'll make love every night!"* Dany's a rough-and-ready boy from the wrong side of the tracks [rough translation: *mal élevé, un air railleur, éffronté*]. I love running my hands through his black, curly hair. Dany's my friend. I love only him, every night. *"Oh, Dany—my Dany! We'll make love all night long! Oh, Dany! Come into my bed!"*

In March, Marcel Cerdan travelled to London, where he fought and won Dick Turpin at Earls Court. In what would be the first of three brief visits to Britain, Piaf accompanied him. She was inundated with offers to perform there, and turned them all down though there were two private recitals at the Mayfair Hotel, her programme the same one as at the Copacabana the previous year. Upon her return to Paris she set about finding an apartment for herself and Cerdan, mindless of the fact that he is reputed to have told her that he would never leave his wife and children. She also wrote a song in his honour, which she only performed twice.

56: *Tu n'as pas besoin de mes rêves* (You don't need my dreams) (Edith Piaf, Marguerite Monnot).
24 April: Tape recording for the radio show *Edith Piaf chante pour vous seul*, released posthumously.
Piano accompaniment: Robert Chauvigny.
The half-spoken, half-sung lyric has Piaf confessing how she used to treat the men in her life, always holding the upper hand and placing each on a pedestal before knocking him off—until the current man in her life—Marcel Cerdan, obviously—causes her to change tactics.

> My head's a box filled with dreams. Smack in the middle, there's a ladder, which I made all the men that pleased me climb. Fearlessly, they climbed very high, obviously while I was holding the ladder. But then I let go of it, and they took a tumble from high up. Then when I was about start all over again, things had changed quite a bit. For *you* don't need my dreams to make me love you. You're laughing as soon as the sun rises, and I've never seen you cry. You sing out loud over some trifle—obviously, you sing badly, but you do it so gently that my heart goes crazy. For *you* don't need my dreams to make me love you. You laugh as soon as the sun rises and

you never make me cry. Yes, things have changed quite a bit. I had to scramble up my ladder, but I was the only one going up, for he watched me from below. Darling, don't let go of the ladder [for] I'd take a tumble from high up, and I don't know what would become of me! You're walking on my ambitions—to hell with my imagination! For *you* don't need my dreams to make me love you. You're laughing as soon as the sun rises, and I've never seen you cry. If by chance I get the sulks [*Si par hasard je fais la tête*], it's crazy how this amuses you so much that this throws me [*j'en suis désarmée*] and my heart remains crazy. For *you* don't need my dreams to make me love you. You're laughing and lifting me up—and I lose all the dignity I have!

Piaf's next recording session saw her cutting one of the songs she had performed on 16 May 1948 as part of her command recital for Princess Elizabeth and Prince Philip, and which she had deliberated about recording until now following complaints that the piece—which ends with the young lovers being mowed down by a car—had been too morose and depressing.

57: *Tous les amoureux chantent* (All the lovers are singing) (Jean Jeepy, Marguerite Monnot).
December: live performance, Copacabana, Paris. Released posthumously.

Accompaniment: Daniel White & His Orchestra.
19 June 1950: Columbia BF 311, A-side.
Accompaniment: Robert Chauvigny & His Orchestra.

> In street, all the lovers are singing street-songs. From above, the sunshine floods them and the crowd and the world drowns in the hubbub. In the street, Suzon and Jean-Pierre are singing street-songs in their own style. She is so blonde—as blonde as a sunbeam. Her wandering curls form halos against the sky. And him—a little local boy, that's all. Barely forty years between them. *"Long live the lovers in the street!"* In the street, all the lovers are singing…But, what's that, in the throng in the street? It's Suzon, running, distraught, without Jean-Pierre! Distraught, in the street, Suzon's weeping for her lover! *"Look out!"* Cars and bicycles are honking! We ring [our bicycle bells], we whistle, we shout, *"Look out!"* A slamming on of brakes! In the street, all the lovers are weeping. High above, the sunshine. Crazy people dancing around—everyone laughing, for the crowd are mocking the lovers who are dying in the street!

Piaf spent much of the summer of this year preparing her third trip to the United States, which as before would begin with a stint at the Versailles. As such there were just two visits to the studio:

58: *Pleure pas* (Don't cry) (Henri Contet, Aimé Barelli).
11 July: Columbia BF 265, B-side.
Accompaniment: Robert Chauvigny & His Orchestra.
Henri Contet (1904-98), Piaf's former lover, who after their split kept on supplying her with some of her most famous songs. Aimé Barelli (1917-95) was the bandleader husband of Piaf's most formidable rival, Lucienne Delyle. For many years, they "borrowed" each other's songs, until their enmity was relaxed somewhat by her writing a song especially for Delyle. Piaf performed this mostly-spoken neurotic piece for the first time on 16 May 1948 as part of her command recital before Princess Elizabeth and Prince Philip. Not to be confused with *Don't Cry*, the English language version of the later *C'est d'a faut à tes yeux*.

> Don't cry. Your eyes are too beautiful for that.
> Don't cry, or I'll cry with you! My poor big boy, I
> can't see that! Be quiet. Your heart's bursting
> [while you're] in my arms! My love, speak to me!
> Tell me! But, my turn first. You'll see that I'm
> crying better than you! Don't cry...When you cry,
> I'm on my Cross. You see, you're making me feel
> bad, and you've no right! Don't cry! My big fellow,
> what's happening? Your heart's not in the same
> place, I can see that. And if you cry, what am I
> going to do? You're sorrowful. My God! Misery!
> And I can do nothing about it! Don't cry...Smile for
> me at least once, then you'll have the right [to cry].
> There! You said something you shouldn't! My love,

that's it! You no longer love me. We only had one love, and your heart lost it. Don't cry—everything changes, comes and goes…You'll see, everything will work out. Why? Well, you see—*I'm* not crying!

59: *L'orgue des amoureux* (The lovers' barrel-organ) (Francis Carco, André Varel, Charlie Bailly).
21 July: Columbia BF 265, A-side.
André Varel (1908-83) was one half (with Charly Bailly, 1921-2010) of the singer-songwriter duo, Varel & Bailly. Poet, *fantaisiste* and author Francis Carco (1886-1958) wrote many songs, perhaps his most famous being *Le doux caboulot*, for Marie Dubas.

The other day, in the yard under my window, an old barrel organ played an old love song. And nothing changed. *Amour* [love] rhymed with *toujours* [always]. Listening to this romance which recalled the past I thought I'd had enough, but alas, it started all over again: "*I gave you my heart…I gave you my life and my happy soul, despite your mocking. All together now: It's yours for life!*" Nevertheless it's true, when I think about it. I loved him madly, and no other lover caused me such torments. And this is my recompense, having believed in his promises [*ses serments*]. It took one mundane adventure, one fine evening, for nature to take its course. I didn't deserve it! "*I gave you my heart…*" What can we do

100

about ourselves? Each of us follows their own path. It's human nature [*le sort de tous les humains*]! But those who go hand-in-hand murmuring "*I love you!*" should be thinking about tomorrow. With a sad tune whose echo swiftly flies off, the [barrel] organ left. And, pardoning the unfaithful man, I sang to console myself: "*I gave you my heart...I gave you my life and my happy soul, despite your mocking. All together now: It's yours for life!*"

60: *Dis-moi, garcon* (Tell me, boy) (Edith Piaf, Robert Chauvigny).
August: tape recording. Registered with Éditions Edimarton. The sheet music was printed. No other details.

61: *What Can I Do?* (Edith Piaf, Harold Rome, Henri Betti).
September: live performance, Versailles, New York, not thought to have been recorded.
The English-language adaptation of *Mais qu'est-ce que j'ai?* No other details.

On 16 June, Marcel Cerdan had returned to New York to defend his title against Jake La Motta, and lost. Work commitments had kept Piaf in Paris, but she had become so anxious over being separated from him that she had written a lyric which Marguerite Monnot had set to music, detailing the scenario, should he die while they were apart! This later became *Hymne à l'amour*, but for now...

62: *Je te retrouverai dans l'éternité* (Edith Piaf, Marguerite Monnot). See also *Hymne à l'amour*.
14 September: live performance, Versailles, New York. As yet, unreleased.
Accompaniment: Robert Chauvigny & His Orchestra.

> Heaven (*le ciel bleu*) may collapse on top of us, and the earth may cave in. It matters little to me, if you love me. I don't give a damn about the whole world! So long as love floods my mornings, so long as my body trembles beneath your hands. I care little for my problems, my love, seeing as you love me! I'll go to the end of the world, I'll dye my hair blonde if you ask me to. I'll take down the moon. I'll steal a fortune if you ask me to. I'll renounce my country, renounce my friends if you ask me to. They can laugh at me—I'll do anything, if you ask me to. If one day, life tears you away from me, if you die while far away from me it won't matter if you love me, for I'll die too! We'll have eternity in the immensity of heaven. In heaven, no more problems. My love—if you die, I will find you again in eternity!

Piaf missed Cerdan so much whilst appearing in New York that she called him and begged him to join her. On 27 October he was photographed at Orly airport with the celebrated violinist Ginette Neveu, just before they boarded the plane for New York. Seven hours later, this crashed into

Mount Rodonta in the Azores, killing everyone on board. Marlene Dietrich remembered that day only too well:

> Only two people were capable of breaking that kind of news to her—myself and her manager [Louis Barrier], who had time to get there only because Edith always slept in until the middle of the afternoon, then rehearsed or received friends until it was time to go onstage. Everyone put on an act until he arrived. God above, she went crazy with grief. I was terrified of leaving her side for a moment. As an act of penance, she cut her hair—I still have the scissors—and she shut herself up in her room until she received a call saying Cerdan's body had been found. It was a terrible thing to have to watch her suffer.

Piaf had been about to go in stage when Marlene broke the news, and refused to cancel the performance. Halfway through her recital, she collapsed after singing *Je te retrouverai dans l'éternité*, but after a few minutes respite in her dressing room, comforted by Marlene she resumed her performance. Henceforth, the number would take on a new meaning: she would always blame herself and don the proverbial hair-shirt for "predicting" her lover's death in a song, which as the later *Hymne à l'amour* would remain an essential part of her repertoire for another decade.

1950

Upon her return to Paris, Piaf revisited the scene of one of her earlier triumphs—the Copacabana—for a three-week engagement. There were no visits to the studio during the first four months of this year and, so far as is known, only two new songs added to Piaf's repertoire—one which was just as quickly removed, and the other which caused some of her closest friends to worry that Marcel Cerdan's death had left her bordering on the point of insanity.

63: *Laisse-le partir* (Let him leave) (Edith Piaf, Robert Chauvigny).
February: live performance, Copacabana. Not recorded.
Accompaniment: Robert Chauvigny & His Orchestra.
Very little is known of this song. It was given a poor reception by the audience, and Piaf eventually gave it to the *fantaisiste* Renée Passeur (1905-75).

64: *Chanson bleue* (Edith Piaf, Marguerite Monnot).
February: live performance, Copacabana, not recorded.
15 April 1951: Columbia BFX 34 (12-inch), A-side.
Accompaniment: Robert Chauvigny & His Orchestra.
Choir: Raymond Saint-Paul.
Along with the Biblical references to Jesus' life, the *bleue* also refers to things heavenly, as opposed to the colour.

I'm going to create a heavenly song for you, that you may have a child's dreams where your nights are no longer tormented. So, by day you may sing, that others might have hope...When the world has learned it [the song], you'll leave life. You'll come to sing it in the heavens. Heavenly song...Recalling your suffering, you will make the angels weep, carrying within your too-lovely hands your heart, your tears, and then your life...When Jesus died on His cross, he suffered as much as you. Forgive your mother and the Good Lord, and leave behind on earth—like God [would]—a heavenly song...There, your mission is finished. Your friends, you will leave them. Caress children's hair. Smile at old folks while on your way. You, who have no tomorrows left...Your sorrowful mornings are over. Saint Peter, the angels and the Good Lord will open the Gates of Heaven for you. Heavenly song...

For over a year, Piaf had requiem masses sung for Cerdan at the church in Auteuil, the ceremony always ending with a choir singing *Chanson bleue*. Such was the weight of emotion that she removed it from her repertoire after this one live performance, and did not record it in the studio for over a year. As such, she would mourn Cerdan for the rest of her life, which from this point rapidly descended into a downward spiral of alcohol and drugs, as if oblivion was the only means of coping with the tragedy. She sought solace in the arms of men, all of them married or gay. Some of them hindered rather than helped her to control her demons. Others were violent towards her, her recompense being that they provided her with some of the finest songs of the post-Cerdan second half of her career, which saw the Piaf legend moving from strength to strength.

The most bizarre element of the Piaf-Cerdan affair and its aftermath was her taking Cerdan's widow, Marinette, and their three children under her wing. Many years later Marcel Cerdan Jr. would portray his father in the film, *Edith et Marcel*, after Patrick Dewaere, the actor contracted for the part, committed suicide. In the meantime, inasmuch as *Chanson bleue* had had such a traumatic effect on her, Piaf initially would have nothing to do with the reworked *Je te retrouverai dans l'éternité*, and as *Hymne à l'amour*, Marguerite Monnot offered it to Yvette Giraud, who turned it down. Jacqueline François subsequently recorded it for Polydor—and when Piaf listened to and denounced the test-pressing of this, she decided to record the song herself. It would become her biggest-seller to date.

65: *Hymne à l'amour* (Edith Piaf, Marguerite Monnot).
2 May 1950: Columbia BF 306, A-side.
July 1951: soundtrack for the film, *Paris chante toujours!*
Accompaniment: Robert Chauvigny & His Orchestra.
Choir: Raymond Saint-Paul.
The lyrics are identical to those of the earlier *Je te retrouverai dans l'éternité*, with the exception of the closing stanza. In the earlier song, there is no musical interlude before Piaf sings the closing lines:

Nous aurons pour nous l'éternité,
Dans le bleu de toute l'immensité,
Mon amour, si tu m'aimes,
Je te retrouverai dans l'éternité!

(We will have eternity in the blue of all immensity,
My love, if you love me,
I'll find you again in eternity!)

At the end of *Hymne à l'amour*, Piaf sings the lines while casting doubts on their relationship...

Dans le ciel, plus de problèmes!
Mon amour, crois-tu qu'on s'aime?

...after which there is a three-bar musical interlude which builds up to a crashing crescendo, where she closes:

Dieu réunit ceux qui s'aiment!

(In heaven, no more problems!
My love, do you think we love each other?
God unites those who love!)

There are numerous live versions between 1955 and 1960 (when Piaf removed the song from her repertoire, along with several others, including *L'accordéoniste*, claiming that their range was too much for her), where she swaps around the final two lines of the song.

66: *Le ciel est fermé.* (Heaven is closed). (Henri Contet, Marguerite Monnot).

19 June: Columbia BF 311, B-side.

Accompaniment: Robert Chauvigny & His Orchestra.

This song with it complicated lyric and key-changes was first performed before Princess Elizabeth and Prince Philip. As with some of the other songs presented that evening, Piaf initially declined to record it, having been told by the organisers that her set-list had been "too maudlin".

> Tired of the people on earth, God, overworked, decided between two mysteries, and decided to call it a day. He extinguished a few stars, closed down heaven, and from a cloud fashioned a sail which was carried away by the wind. And here we are! The sun is lopsided, all the men walk around with their heads hanging down, the earth spins around the other way, and the sea gets annoyed and leaves! But the prayers keep on mounting....Prayers asking for nothing, queuing up, waiting for God! And that's why [the people] are annoyed. Their prayers are no longer asked for by God! And as they have nothing to do [the people] confide in each other.

Then, in the spoken section of the song, the one posing and replying to the questions assumes the role of God:

> *"Why have you come?"*
> *"I've come on behalf of someone called Romeo and*

a certain Juliet!"

"What are they doing to annoy people, on earth? Can't they let them love each other in peace? Not easy to arrange, their story! And....you?"

"Me, for a boy who's in big trouble with the taxman!"

"I don't see how I can do much for him! And you?"

"Me...professional secrecy!"

"And you, over there?"

"I'm here on behalf of a madman. Well, a poet. It's the same thing!"

"Firstly, what he's demanding of the world is impossible. And preaching kindness is impossible!"

"Tell us [why]*! Maybe it's funny!"*

"If you wish. In any case, it'll change nothing..."

"I know very well how to upset you. But it's like this. I need you. Please lend me the angels! There should be a few everywhere! For the sun, one per person! And for love, please fill men's hands with love so that they can make big bouquets!"

The melody resumes—though the final lines are ominous:

Thus God returned. Thunder was unemployed. The sun passed overhead and the earth began spinning the right way around! *"Open the doors so that the sun shines in the wheat-fields—so that the world can finally turn without trembling!"* And love grew in the fields! And men harvested whilst singing, and

109

lovers will never die again because everyone in the world loved each other! …Such a pity for the girls and boys, though—that all of this is but a song!

67: *La fête continue* (The fair raves on). (Michel Emer).
20 June: Columbia BF 319, A-side.
13 January 1957: live in French & English, Carnegie Hall, New York.
Accompaniment: Robert Chauvigny & His Orchestra.
In America, Piaf announced this song with: "*I know that people have their problems and even tragedies, but I want to close my eyes to all that because tonight I'm going to the fair with my sweetheart, and I want to be happy!*" The music may be lively, but the lyrics are anything but: child-beating, suicide, a road accident and the ambulance turning up in the section marked [[ ]] which was removed from the final recording.

The fair raves on. Music, roundabouts, nougat, shooting-ranges, fortune-tellers, nude women. From morning until night it's one long parade! Songs, swings, the fair raves on! On the ground floor, kids are bawling. The father's ill, the mother's left. He clouts the brats and the noise from the fair covers their cries. On an upper floor are two youngsters. You can see how much they're in love! But their parents are against them [*ne veulent rien savoir*]. They've decided to make love just the same, then kill themselves later tonight! Above them, there's a

110

widow. Nothing interests her any more. She only had one son. He was her whole life. He disappeared with the cash-register, since when she weeps day and night. The little boy has got home from school. He got a zero, and is sad because instead of going to the fair next Sunday he'll be staying home. The fair goes on…Opposite are two old people who are nice enough. Twenty-five years ago they lost their daughter. They have just one fad—table-turning [visiting a spiritualist]. *"Spirit—are you there?"* [The table knocks twice] and they are content!

[[At the crossroads, a long car. A newspaper boy on a bike, not looking where he's going. Perhaps it's a fracture. The ambulance takes him away.]]

Like everyone else I watch these dramas, but close my eyes and think of my happiness. We're devoted, body and soul, too happy to care. The fair raves on!

68: *Il fait bon t'aimer* (It's good, loving you). (Jacques Plante, Norbert Glanzberg).
20 June: Columbia BF 338, A-side.
Accompaniment: Robert Chauvigny & His Orchestra.

One day when I was feeling sad, you shattered it by taking my tears in your hands and said, "You're too beautiful for these jewels!" For you, I learned how to smile and, since that day understood how one can fear death, when one already knows heaven! It's so good, loving you. You seem to be made for this. To be snuggled up, eyes closed, your head in the crook of my arms. Your lips call so strongly for my kisses. I don't need to force myself. I just have to let myself be rocked, and everything becomes light. It's so good, loving you! Close to you, I'm no longer afraid. I feel so well, sheltered. You closed the door on unhappiness. It won't come in any more—you're stronger than it! And when I go through the streets I carry my voice in my eyes, as if your kisses are following me, and people turn around. It's so good, loving you...

69: *Le chevalier de Paris* (The knight of Paris) (Michel Philippe-Gérard, Angele Vannier).
20 June: Columbia BF 338, B-side.
Accompaniment: Robert Chauvigny & His Orchestra.
The song was awarded the Grand Prix du Disque, in 1952, after which Piaf declared it "too commercial" and removed it from her repertoire. English lyrics to Philippe-Gérard's composition were provided by Johnny Mercer in 1951. Bing Crosby was the first to record it, followed by Peggy Lee, and by Marlene Dietrich (as *Die Welt war jung*) with German words by Max Colpet. The music suggests a medieval setting, but the action is contemporary, and in the English and German language versions, Mercer and Colpet capture the essence of the original: the man (aka *le grand chevalier*) from the country village who arrives in Paris and

falls in with the wrong crowd, but who eventually learns the error of his reprobate ways whilst reflecting upon better days, and upon one girl in particular. Thus he returns to his village so that they may be reunited, enabling him to wager another kind of war [*la guerre en dentelles*]—that of love!

In the heart of Paris, the great knight no longer recalled the essence of the prairies. He waged war with his friends—in the smoke, the metros, the cobblestones and bistros. He didn't realise when he was drunk, how he slept standing up. Paris had grabbed him by the scruff of the neck.

Then he reflects upon what he has left behind:

Ah, the apple trees—the country dances and tunes. "I'm not afraid of wolves," the beauty sang. "They're not wicked towards children who have faithful hearts and innocence [*les genoux blancs*]!"

He recalls their meeting, one dew-kissed sunny morning. He was under an apple tree, when she crossed before him:

"Long live the songs of sweethearts! I remember her, with her velvety blood! Her hands spoke of love! She braided the clay with the clouds and pressed the wind against her face, expressing the essence of her journey!" Ah, the apple trees—the country dances and tunes...

113

And realising what he has been missing, he returns to his former life:

> "*Goodbye, Paris,*" said the knight. "*For* [what seems like] *a hundred years, I've slept standing up and without eating the silver apples of my apple trees!*" So the village cried out loud, and all the girls ran outside. But the knight waved to no one but her, with her velvet blood and her heart so true. [And from now on] the knight will only wage war in lace!

70: *C'est de la faute* (It's because of) (Edith Piaf, Robert Chauvigny) *
7 July: Columbia BF 388, B-side.
Accompaniment: Robert Chauvigny & His Orchestra.
* The title on this record label, in later releases listed as *C'est d'la faute de tes yeux* (It's because of your eyes). In this one, Piaf speaks firstly to her dead lover, then explains to her defence lawyer, why she killed him, one assumes because she suspected him of cheating on her.

> I had so much love for a man. He had so little for me. In short, life's a little thing. I killed him—too bad for me! "*All this, it's because of his eyes—the warmth of the mornings, his body next to mine! All this, it's because of the fine days. Because of love, the sky was too blue!*" The lawyer defending me recalled our story to prove my innocence, and soiled our finest days. The judge was stern. His vision was

blinkered [*Ses yeux n'avaient pas d'horizon*]. In a deep voice, and without anger, he sent me to prison. *"All this it's because of my eyes. They saw my sorrow dancing within yours. And they saw my love weeping on my blue sky!"*

When Piaf first met Charles Aznavour in 1948, he was one half of the popular Aznavour-Roche duo. Upon learning that he wrote his own songs, she asked him to write one for her. With his partner Pierre Roche he came up with the previously mentioned *Il pleut* (**#34**, **#45**), which she now told him she had hated! Shortly after Marcel Cerdan's death, he presented with *Je hais les dimanches*, which he had written with future Piaf stalwart, Florence Véran. Piaf turned this down and told him to give it to Juliette Gréco, the darling of the Existentialists who not only had a hit with it—really rubbing salt into her wounds, it won her the newly launched *Prix Edith Piaf*. Charles explained to me:

> She went crazy! Though she was always polite whenever they met, Piaf disliked Gréco intensely at this time, accusing her not just of stealing this song from her, but of stealing some of her other songs, including *Les feuilles mortes, Sous le ciel de Paris* and *Chanson de Catherine*. But she promised that she would forgive *me* so long as I wrote her something else.

In the spring of 1950, her first move in coaxing him to split from Roche and pursue a solo career, Piaf roped him into her provincial tour, to be followed by an extensive tour of Canada and the United States. She needed him by her side, she said, to keep her supplied with new material—unlike most of her contemporaries, she did not stick to the same set-list night after night. And as with *Je hais les dimanches*, most of the songs he presented to her were rejected, and given to others: Juliette Gréco, Lucienne Delyle and Patachou, causing Piaf to dislike the first two more than ever, through no fault of their own, though she got along well with Patachou—for now. Charles recalled:

> I wasn't going to spend hours—sometimes days—working on a song, only to throw it into the trash because Piaf didn't like it. And of course, when they recorded one of the songs she'd turned down—especially if it was a hit—she went *really* crazy! That's when I used to lock myself in my room! And then I gave her *C'est un gars*, which she accepted only because it was the right song, at the right time, and liked—until Lucienne recorded it!

71: *C'est un gars* (It's a boy) (Aznavour-Roche).
7 July: Columbia BF 330, A-side.
Accompaniment: Robert Chauvigny & His Orchestra.

> The soles of my shoes are dropping off, my dress so threadbare you can see through it [*Sous mes pieds mes semelles se dérobent…On voit le jour à travers*

116

ma robe]. My bodice is patched up, my effects worn out. Who cares what they say round about? I don't care about the rest of the world! It's a boy who came into my life, a boy who said crazy things. *"You're pretty—pretty!"* No one's ever said that to me! He's a boy who looks like an angel—who speaks like the angels. *"You're pretty—pretty!"* I'm all dizzy! Since my childhood I've dwelled in the black streets of ignorance. Suddenly, everything lit up. My heart began to sing! It's beautiful, the love that walks around with a handsome boy holding the chain. One wishes to remain prisoner just to contemplate one's jailor! It's a boy who came into my life, a boy who said crazy things. *"You're pretty—pretty! Do you want me for life?"* "YES!!!!"*

The new man in Piaf's life—the first after Cerdan—was neither a *"gars"* nor an angel. Eddie Constantine (1917-93) was a brash American actor-singer—like Cerdan not appealing to look at, with a pock-marked face, but with a sexy smile and an affable disposition. Like the others, he was married. Having failed to get into Hollywood musicals, he had left his wife and small daughter and headed for Europe, promising to return to his family once he had made a name for himself. His first six months in France had seen him doing a number of "non-showbusiness" jobs, including washing corpses in a funeral parlour. His singing career had taken off, but only in a small way, when an agent had taken him on as a *"dernière minute"*, filling in for cancellations at

117

Left Bank cabarets. At one of these he had been "spotted" by Lucienne Boyer, and offered a regular spot at her Club de l'Opéra. While here, he had written an English lyric for *Hymne à l'amour*, which he had taken to Piaf. Initially, she had been suspicious of the man—nothing to do with him being married, for she did not find this out for some time—but because he informed her that on the day that Cerdan's death had been announced, *he* had been celebrating his thirty-second birthday with friends and had been unmoved by news of the tragedy. She soon came around, and included the song in her next recording session—the first of two which saw her laying down some of the songs she would be performing in English for American audiences.

72: *Hymn To Love* (Edith Piaf, Marguerite Monnot, Eddie Constantine.
8 July: Columbia (USA) 39027, A-side.
Accompaniment: Robert Chauvigny & His Orchestra.
Choir: Raymond Saint-Paul.
The English-language version of *Hymne à l'amour*, which Piaf dropped from her repertoire the following year, after she had ended her relationship with Eddie Constantine. In the meantime, she announced that Constantine would be augmenting not just her provincial tour, but that she would be taking him to America. She was still unaware that he was married, and could leave her at any time and return to his family. There would also be another Aznavour song, which she decided would be the B-side of *C'est un gars*.

73: *La Vie En Rose* (Edith Piaf, Louiguy, Mack David).
8 July (Version 1): Columbia (USA) 38948, A-side.
8 July (Version 2), released posthumously.
Accompaniment: Robert Chauvigny & His Orchestra.
The English-language version of *La vie en rose.* Version 2, has a heavy drumbeat throughout the second refrain which interferes with Piaf's vocals. Previously, there had been two different versions of the song, using the same melody but different lyrics. *You're Too Dangerous, Cheri* (**#48**), which Piaf performed live for a brief period, and *Take Me To Your Heart Again,* which she was offered but rejected. Both versions were covered by Gracie Fields. New York-born Mack David (1912-93) had previously worked on Disney films such as *Alice in Wonderland* and *Cinderella.* He supplied lyrics to over 1,000 songs, but it was *La vie en rose* which put him on the international map, and he went on to adapt several more Piaf songs, and classics such as Gilbert Bécaud's *Seule sur son étoile,* which as *It Must Be Him* became a million-seller for Vikki Carr. His brother, Hal (1920-2012), later collaborated with Burt Bacharach.

74: *The Three Bells* (Jean Villard, Bert Reisfeld).
8 July: Columbia (USA) 38948, B-side.
Accompaniment: Robert Chauvigny & His Orchestra.
Choir: Raymond Saint-Paul.
The English-language version of *Les trois cloches*, wherein Jean-Francois Nicot becomes Jimmy Brown. The refrain (*C'est pour accueillir une âme*...etc, in the original) appears

only after the last verse in Piaf's English version. In some cover versions of the song, it is re-titled *The Jimmy Brown Song*.

75: *Just Across The Way* (Michel Émer, Christopher Hassall).
8 July: Tape recording or acetate.
The English-language version of *De l'autre côté de la rue*. The first Piaf song to be adapted into English—in 1944, for Elisabeth Welch. It is not known if Piaf sang it on stage, but it does appear to have been recorded, according to the National Library of Australia, though it is yet to surface. Christopher Hassall (1912-63) was an English actor and lyricist famed for his working partnership with Ivor Novello. The lyric partly reads:

> Close by the fish-and-chip shop,
> Posh people never use,
> Step through some sort of hoarding
> And through a kind of Mews…
> Just across the way there's a rich girl who's in clover…
> Wishing she could be just like me…

76: *Simply A Waltz* (Norman Wallace).
10 July: Columbia USA 39027, B-side.
Accompaniment: Robert Chauvigny & His Orchestra.
Piano: Norman Wallace.
Piaf sang this, along with *Autumn Leaves*, before Dwight D

Eisenhower at a command performance. He later declared that it was his favourite song of all time. It is only one of two Piaf songs (the other is *I Remember Today*) to have never been sung in French. Chicago-born Norman Wallace (1924-70) was a renowned singer-lounge pianist.

77: *Il y avait* (There was). (Charles Aznavour, Pierre Roche).
10 July: Columbia BF 330, B-side.
Accompaniment: Robert Chauvigny & His Orchestra.

> There was a boy who lived a simple life, working in the suburbs...a girl who dreamed wisely while awaiting love...a spring of romance passing by, searching for troubled hearts to lend its promises to and make them fall in love. There was a wonderful moment when their eyes met—those delicious moments when without saying anything they understood one another. There was Fate which pushed the boy into taking her hand. There was the warmth of happiness which rose within their hearts. There was that furnished room, its windows overlooking the courtyard—the couple making love, and their phrases speaking of forever. There was the kid who walked his hand through the flaxen hair of the girl with dreamy eyes while happiness installed itself within their hearts. There were those two bodies, lost in happiness and unparalleled joy—all of those lost dreams replacing their sleepless nights.

For the lovers, however, bliss is short-lived:

> There was the moment when spring suddenly took back its promises—when happiness fled in tears, having broken two hearts. There was the boy who lived the simple life, working in the suburbs...the girl who wept, dreaming of her first love. There was Fate, walking along its way, and doing nothing—for as long as there are lovers, there will be promises that last for but one spring.

78: *All My Love* (Paul Durand, Mitchell Parish).
10 July, Tape recording.
Accompaniment: Robert Chauvigny & His Orchestra.
As *Boléro*, this had French lyrics by Piaf's former lover Henri Contet and was written for the French film, *Scandale aux Champs-Élysées* (see **#36**) where it was performed by Jacqueline François, though Lucienne Delyle had the biggest hit with it in France. Piaf performed it several times in the United States before giving it to Patti Paige, who took it to the top of the hit-parade, her first US #1.

79: *My Lost Melody* [2] (Raymond Asso, Marguerite Monnot, Mack David).
10 July: unreleased.
Accompaniment: Robert Chauvigny & His Orchestra.
The second of the three English-language versions of *Je n'en connais pas la fin*. At 3:07 shorter than the later recording, it opens with the French refrain, before she sings

122

David's lyric, in keeping with the Asso original, part of which reads:

> When twilight shadows are aglow,
> I hear a song I used to know…
> Leaving a spell of long ago.
> It seems to bring a melody of the lost love that used to be…

Though this recording has never been commercially released, it turns up regularly on social media channels such as youtube.

Charles Aznavour recalled of the provincial tour, which took up much of the summer:

> The French tour was a nightmare. I opened the show. The rest of the time I was the dogsbody—I drove the car, ran errands, carried suitcases, and was cursed at all the time, and I loved every minute of it because all the time I was with Piaf, I was learning. Her English was not that bad, but she made him [Eddie Constantine] learn French, and his accent was terrible. The critics hated him, and she took it out on me.

The American tour, which as per usual kicked off with a season at the Versailles, in New York, was a sell-out. Piaf would have liked to have stayed longer in the United States but she had commitments in Paris—more studio work, and her first musical-comedy, *La p'tite Lili*. Her final performance before leaving for France was on NBC Radio's *The Big Show*, hosted by Tallulah Bankhead.

80: *Autumn Leaves* (Jacques Prévert, Joseph Kosma, Johnny Mercer)
24 December: live on NBC Radio's *The Big Show*.
Accompaniment: Meredith Wilson, His Orchestra & Choir.
30 December: Columbia USA 39135, B-side.
13 January 1957: live, Carnegie Hall, New York.
Accompaniment (12/50 and 1/57): Robert Chauvigny & His Orchestra. Choir unknown.
The song was written in 1946 for the soundtrack of the film *Les portes de la nuit*, when it was sung by Yves Montand and the soprano Irène Joachim. The first commercial recordings, several months ahead of Piaf, were by Montand, and Cora Vaucaire. The first artiste to record the English language version, in July 1950, was Jo Stafford. Piaf does not sing the lengthy French introduction and verse, just the English refrain, alternated with the French refrain, which translates thus:

> It's a song which resembles us. You loved me, I loved you. We lived together…you who loved me, I who loved you. But life separates the ones who love, sweetly, noiselessly. And the sea erases the footsteps of the disunited lovers from the sand.

81: *Il est né, le divin enfant* (He is born, the divine child). (Traditional).
Accompaniment: Meredith Wilson & His Orchestra.
24 December: live on NBC Radio's *The Big Show*.
A traditional French Christmas carol, this begins with a bar from *The First Noël*.

> He is born, the divine child! Play, oboes! Vibrate, pipes! He is born, the divine child! Let us sing his coming! For more than four-thousand years, he was promised to us by the prophets. We've been waiting for this happy time. He is born, the divine child! Let us sing his coming!

82: *My Lost Melody* [3] (Harold Rome, Raymond Asso, Marguerite Monnot).
30 December: Columbia USA 39135, A-side
The slightly longer, re-arranged version (4:43) of **#52**
The BBC used it as an opener for their radio series, *Portrait of Piaf*, presented by Elisabeth Welch in May 1976.

83: *If You Go* (Michel Emer, Geoffrey Parsons)
30 December: Tape recording.
The English-language adaptation *of Si tu partais*. Piaf sang this infrequently during various American tours, but later confessed to never having been keen on the English lyrics. There was an excellent cover-version by Vera Lynn, and in 1961 Peggy Lee recorded it for the album of the same name, unaware who had created it. She recalled:

Had I known it was Piaf's song, I would have asked her permission to sing it at once. Then I heard on the grapevine that she may have been displeased with me because she had also sung *All The Apple Trees*. I didn't know that either! So I asked her if I could do *If You Go*, and she replied that if I did, it would be a great honour for her. Coming from a great lady like her, *I* was the one who felt honoured!

84: *Don't Cry* (Edith Piaf, Eddie Constantine).
30 December: Columbia USA 39211, A-side.
Accompaniment: Robert Chauvigny & His Orchestra. Choir unknown.
The English-language adaptation of *C'est de la faute*, though Constantine's albeit effective lyrics have nothing to do with those of the original.

85: *Chante-moi (Darling Sing To Me)* (Edith Piaf, Mack David).
30 December: Version 1: Columbia USA 39211, B-side.
1956: Version 2 (released posthumously)
Accompaniment: Robert Chauvigny & His Orchestra. Choir unknown. Solo voice: Marcel Jiteau.
The English adaptation of *Chante-moi*, already written with words and music by Piaf, but which would not be recorded until the following year. The first version has a mandolin introduction, whereas the one archived (but only during Piaf's lifetime) does not.

86: *Cause I Love You* (Edith Piaf, Rick French).
30 December: Columbia USA 39320, A-side. *
Accompaniment: Robert Chauvigny & His Orchestra.
While in the United States, Piaf had rehearsed some of the songs for *La p'tite Lili*, for one of which—*Du matin jusqu'au soir*—she had written words and music. Little is known of Rick French, who went on to adapt several more Piaf songs into English, and who is more or less faithful to the original lyric with this one.

87: *I Shouldn't Care* (Michel Emer, Rick French).
30 December: Columbia USA 39320, B-side. *
Accompaniment: Robert Chauvigny & His Orchestra.
The English adaptation of *Je m'en fous pas mal*, which, though compelling, unlike Rick French's previous adaptation has nothing in common with Michel Emer's lyric other than the title.
* These two songs have erroneously been listed as recorded at Paris' Pathé-Marconi Studios on 14/15 December, but this was not possible as Piaf was in the United States on this date.

Piaf with Marcel Cerdan.

With Charles Aznavour.

With Eddie Constantine.

1951

La p'tite Lili, scripted by Marcel Achard (1899-1974) and with music by Marguerite Monnot, opened at the ABC on 15 February 1951. The tension was immense, from the first day of rehearsals. Achard, one of France's top playwrights and a man of considerable clout, had asked for the ABC because it was then the most important music-hall in Paris. The problem lay with its tetchy Roumanian director, Mitty Goldin (1895-1956). Most of the songs had been written the previous year—some by Achard, some by Piaf for Eddie Contantine, and others by Charles Aznavour, though none of them had been aired publicly. She therefore demanded that both men be included in the production. Goldin fought against this. He disliked Aznavour, and deemed Constantine's French so dire that audiences would not understand what he was saying or singing about. He absolutely loathed Piaf: the pair had clashed swords when she had appeared here during her Raymond Asso days, to such an extent that he had sworn then never to allow her in his theatre again. The fact that *La p'tite Lili* would be a guaranteed sell-out, earning him a lot of money, enabled Goldin to change his mind—and it was *he* who stayed away from his own theatre not just while rehearsals were under way, but for the entire run of the production. There were also problems between Constantine and the second lead, Robert Lamoureux (1920-2011), when the press began speculating that he and Piaf were lovers, though this does not appear to have been true.

88: *Demain, il fera jour* (Tomorrow will be another day) (Marcel Achard, Marguerite Monnot). From *La p'tite Lili.*
6 April: Columbia BF 370, A-side.
Accompaniment: Robert Chauvigny & His Orchestra.
Choir: Raymond Saint-Paul.

> Tomorrow will be another day. It's when all is hopeless that everything begins...After love, another love begins. Tomorrow, the little boy will come, whistling. His arms will be filled with springtime. Tomorrow, you'll see the shining of the honeymoon. The bells will be ringing in your heaven! For tomorrow you'll smile again, love again, suffer again—for ever! Tomorrow will be another day. In your heart, broken for ever, love still remains. You think that your grief is so profound that your life will end there. The most beautiful girl in the world can always give more than she has. Tomorrow will be another day. It's when all is lost that everything begins...

89: *Du matin jusqu'au soir* (From morning until night) (Edith Piaf). From *La p'tite Lili.*
11 April: Columbia BF 371, A-side.
Accompaniment: Robert Chauvigny & His Orchestra.
Choir: Raymond Saint-Paul.
15 April: live from Orly airport. Piano: Marguerite Monnot.
Previously recorded in English as *Cause I Love You.* Eddie Constantine has erroneously been cited as lyricist but Piaf's

131

name is listed in the archives and on the label.

> From morning until night, night until morning, I
> love him! What he says, what he does, I find this
> perfect! From daybreak, these are words of love:
> "*My love, we will always love each other!*" He
> smiles and says, "*You turn my life upside-down!*"
> It's that he loves me! It's good to be in love, above
> all when there are two of us, and we love each
> other! "*I love you, you love me, we love each other
> from morning until night, night until morning!*"

Piaf/Lili then explains to the audience, lamely, that she is
not obsessed with her lover, before repeating the refrain:

> I'm not at all blinded by love. I see the pros and
> cons objectively. You can honestly see that I'm
> unbiased...but I frankly confess that there are no
> two like him! From morning until night, and from
> night until morning I love him...we love each other!

90: *L'homme que j'aimerai* (The man I'll love) (Marcel
Achard, Marguerite Monnot). From *La p'tite Lili*.
11 April: Columbia BF 375, B-side.
Accompaniment: Robert Chauvigny & His Orchestra.
In this one, Lili/Piaf tries but fails to sound confident. The
phrase "*de petit vin blanc*" refers to *Le petit vin blanc* (The
small glass of white wine!) recorded by Lina Margy in
1943, and still popular at Bastille Day celebrations.

The man I'll love, I've loved for such a long time. When I get him, I swear to you that I'll keep him. At least I'll try. Men are all the same. In the case of we two, we'll try to be happy. The man I'll love, I've only seen him in my dreams. The twelfth of April already. When will my lover come? He has immense white hands which only caress afterwards [after making love]. A heart like the Fourteenth of July, full of firecrackers [bangers] and romances, of *de petit vin blanc* and romances, a heart made for snuggling up to—so big that I can't get back out of it! The man I'll love, I've loved for such a long time. When he sees me, I'm sure he'll recognise me. He'll whisper, *"You're always the same!"* Then both of us will perhaps be happy. But when I get the lover I'm dreaming about, I'll think about the day I'll lose him. The man I'll love…

91: *Avant l'heure* (Before the appointed time) (Marcel Achard, Marguerite Monnot). From *La p'tite Lili*.
13 April: Columbia BF 370, B-side.
Accompaniment: Robert Chauvigny & His Orchestra.
This songs refers to *Cinq à sept*—a French metonym for the two hours (popular then, but not so much nowadays) when a Frenchman would visit his mistress, between leaving work and arriving home for dinner. Thus, if one arrived early, the husband might still be there, and if one arrived late there was the danger of the husband coming home and catching the adulterers in the act.

Before the appointed time and after the appointed time is no longer the right time! I met him a little too late. He'd already met Germaine. He's been in love with me for five weeks. I didn't give a damn about the quarter-hour [if she was early or late]. Then one day, I understood! He lied to me for three more weeks. Then he went to see Germaine. Ah, my little ones! What have I gotten myself into? [*Qu'est-ce que j'ai pris?*] I don't want him! What am I to do about this? Before…after the appointed time isn't the right time! If one says a quarter-to, it has to be a quarter-to! I met him a little too late!

Piaf then explains the complications of *Cinq à sept*:

Pierre loves Jean's wife. Jean loves Pierre's wife. Pierre's wife loves a sergeant. Jean's wife loves a public official. What are these poor people hoping for? If Pierre's wife had seen the sergeant before meeting Pierre…if Jean's wife had seen the public official before meeting Jean, it would have been another story! There would be happiness in Nogent, instead of tears! The appointed time is the right time…when one says a quarter-to, it has to be a quarter to! I met got there too late!

92: *Si, si, si* (Yes, yes, yes) (Marcel Achard, Marguerite Monnot). From *La p'tite Lili*.

13 April: Columbia BF 372, B-side.

Accompaniment: Robert Chauvigny & His Orchestra.
Duet with Eddie Constantine.
Constantine, aka Spencer the gangster, tells Lili about the girl he loves (his mouse), while she responds sarcastically, and he argues each response with "*Si, si, si, si!*".

SPENCER: Mademoiselle, my lover is as wise as the day of my first Communion. Mademoiselle, my happiness is as strange as a flower one does not know the name of. Mademoiselle, my future is as tender as a memory, as lovely as a song.

LILI: She can't be as good as all that....You have to get to know her. You *don't* know her!....A girl as beautiful as she is can't be wise as well!....The girls around these parts are unfaithful!....I'd worry if I were you, because she's got you under the thumb [*elle te tient à sa merci!*]!

SPENCER: Mademoiselle, my future is as tender as a memory—a glove which retains her perfume. Mademoiselle, my happiness is as rare as a trotting horse that comes in at forty-to-one. Mademoiselle, my love is as simple as the day—the day when two become only one.

LILI: She can't be all that good!....You're annoying me! I've laughed enough! Be happy with your mouse!

93: *Rien de rien* (Nothing at all) (Charles Aznavour, Pierre Roche). From *La p'tite Lili*.
13 April: Columbia BF 371, B-side.

Accompaniment: Robert Chauvigny & His Orchestra.
The "eavesdropping" song, as during the play, Lili walks around the stage spying on lovers.

Nothing at all! Nothing ever happens for me. I ask myself why. Nothing!....From first thing in a morning until bedtime all's quiet and banal. I'd like something fishy to happen—something unexpected. It's not normal! Nothing happens! Here's a couple—whispering, sneaking into a room. I'm guessing a tender adventure, but they're sleeping apart [*ils vont chacun d'leur côté*]!....Nothing! Two men speak in a low voice. Animated chatter. I change places to listen, but alas I only hear "*Yes...No!*"....Nothing! Nothing happens! What's not happening, I would like to happen, but only for me—then I'd be able to see what's happening, and say it's *not* happening! Nothing!....Nothing happens for me!

94: *La valse de l'amour* [1 & 2] (The waltz of love) (Edith Piaf, Marguerite Monnot). From *La p'tite Lili*.
13 April: Version 1: Columbia BF 375, A-side.
15 April: Version 2: released posthumously.
Accompaniment: Robert Chauvigny & His Orchestra.

It's the waltz of love that they're singing in the suburbs. The romance that each one dances to while

136

awaiting love. There's always one heart searching for another....Thus begins a romance! It's the waltz of love!....He lived right across from her—she lived right across from him. He thought, *"Oh, my God! She's beautiful!"* She thought, *"There's no one better than him!"* It's the waltz of love!....There's always a boy for a girl—always a girl for a boy. So long as the girl is kind, the story works out in a tender way. It's the waltz of love!

95: *Petite si jolie* (Little one, so pretty) (Edith Piaf, Marguerite Monnot). From *La p'tite Lili*.
15 April: Columbia BF 372, A-side.
Performed by Eddie Constantine in near-incomprehensible French, though his command of the language would improve considerably over the coming years. Therefore paraphrasing (and sometimes even guess-work) is required in parts of the song.

Little one so pretty, what do you want from me? I love life so much, thinking only of myself. I'm an egotist—I had childhood dreams. If only I could be an artiste, but I have no talent. I'll never have anything, never become anything, or be anybody. I have so little soul. Since childhood I've dreamed of travelling as I watched my mother crying. I'll never be any good, so I'll leave. So there, pretty little thing, you must not cry. You're sad too quickly, and I must be on my way. Goodbye, pretty little one!

96: *C'est toi* (It's you) [1] (Edith Piaf, Robert Chauvigny).

15 April: Columbia BFX 34 (12-inch), B-side.

Duet with Eddie Constantine. From *La p'tite Lili.*

Accompaniment: Robert Chauvigny & His Orchestra.

Choir: Raymond Saint-Paul.

In this, Constantine's French is slightly better—the lyrics being more simplistic—and his harmonising with Piaf exceptional. The song ends with Constantine singing the final refrain in English.

LILI: It's you that I sing about in my songs, you for whom I'm losing my mind. For you, my love, just for you! It's you who makes my days heavenly. It's you—you'll see it in my eyes!

BOTH: It's you, my love, only you!

LILI: Our love's like a beautiful dream. Hear the song as it rises! It dances in your life and in mine…

BOTH: Just like a Viennese waltz!

LILI: It's you that I sing about in my songs…The Good Lord, who does things so well, made us meet each other. He had his reasons, I suppose, for making us fall in love.

SPENCER: It's you that I sing about in my songs, you for whom I'm losing my mind…

[in English] My heart knows the love I feel for you! My heart knows that I will ere be true…

BOTH: It's you, my love. It's you and me! It's you, only you!

97: *Dans tes yeux* (In your eyes) (Edith Piaf, Marguerite Monnot). From *La p'tite Lili*.

15 April: Columbia BF 440, A-side.

Performed by Eddie Constantine, released in 1952 with *Ma main a besoin de ta main* on the B-side.

Accompaniment: Robert Chauvigny & His Orchestra.

> In your eyes I see reflections of Paris. My blue sky, your sky of grey...I see laughs and sorrows, I see the hopes of each of us. And the love of the girls, the desires and dreams of the boys...In your eyes, I see springtime in Paris—its blue sky, its grey sky. And this is why I'm in love with you.

From this point, the middle section of the song defies translation, with Constantine singing *"la-la-la"* when he forgets the words, and appearing to tell his girl that her face reminds him of the local town hall! It ends with him tunelessly shouting about "Broadway" and *Night and Day*. Upon Piaf's instruction the song was dropped from *La p'tite Lili* halfway through the run, not included on the album, and the 78 rpm recording was released only when Constantine was out of the picture.

On 4 July, according to Charles Aznavour, Piaf and Constantine had a massive row which saw her refusing to attend an Independence Day celebration he had organised, and head for the Pathé-Marconi studios instead to record two songs which she had been singing for a while:

When Piaf said *"Jump!"* everyone jumped. She called the studio and said she was on her way, which meant that anyone using the slot that she wanted had to be shunted aside. When she was feeling down in the dumps, to cheer herself up she would call me or Michel Émer and say, *"Hey—write me a song and make sure you find me a new way to die!"* Michel was good at that, whereas I preferred to write about being alive. She always said that *Une enfant* was her favourite out of all songs I wrote for her. That's because someone died at the end—in this instance an errant child who is found dead at the side of the road, as opposed to the usual drowning, murder, electricity, gas or routine broken heart.

98: *Une enfant* (A child) (Charles Aznavour)
4 July: Columbia BF 386, B-side.
Accompaniment: Robert Chauvigny & His Orchestra.
Choir: Raymond Saint-Paul.

A child of sixteen. A child of springtime. Lying on the road. She lived in one of those neighbourhoods were everyone is stinking rich [*riche à crever*]. She left her parents to follow a bohemian boy who knew only too well how to say, *"I love you!"* It became overwhelming, and their sunny hearts left without leaving an address, taking with them just their youth, and the sweetness of their sin.....Their hearts knew no seasons, and didn't want prison [for being under-aged]. They lived from day to day, never staying in the same place. Their hearts needed space to contain such love. Her present and future was his magnificent love which rocked her like a canticle and saw her eyes lost in heaven [*le bleu*]....But his love was too great for the child's soul, and she was ruled by her heart [*elle ne vivait que par son cœur*], a heart which made its own world. But God doesn't accept worlds that he hasn't created! Love being their only banquet, he deserted her for a few crumbs [aka, a cheap fling]. Thus her life went into decline and the child knew hunger. A child of sixteen, of springtime. Lying on the road...dead!

99: *Chante-moi* (Sing to me) (Edith Piaf).
4 July: Columbia BF 386, A-side.
Accompaniment: Robert Chauvigny & His Orchestra. Solo voice: Marcel Jiteau.
Written and performed (but not recorded) before the English version of the same title (**#85**) this has the same mandolin introductions.

I told the boy who was singing in my street for lost hearts, the boy who searched within my heart with his unhappy voice: "*Sing me love-songs, pretty melodies! Sing life's song to me at daybreak! Sing of my nights of love! If you can, sing about happiness...all the words of love, so that the sorrow within my heart will dance away!"* And the voice of the boy, singing in my street for lost hearts, searched within my heart to find happiness and sang the most beautiful love-song! I listened to the pretty melody, and I saw the day break and love lit up my life! He sang about my nights of love...he even sang bout happiness! And love, making a detour, chased the sorrow from my heart!

Despite the immense success of *La p'tite Lili*—every performance a sell-out, with the ABC installing folding seats in the aisles—few of the songs stood up on their own extant of the scenario, and none were performed on the stage by Piaf, after the final curtain. None of the 78rpm recordings were hits and the 10-inch vinyl album (FL 9535) released only in the United States, was a flop. Piaf's relationship with Eddie Constantine floundered when his wife arrived in Paris, though another was waiting in the wings to take his place—not Robert Lamoureux, as everyone predicted, but the racing cyclist André Pousse, who in turn would be replaced by his team-mate, Louis "Toto" Gérardin. More drama followed in the middle of August when, with Pousse at the wheel, Piaf suffered two broken ribs and a fractured arm in a car-crash. She refused to be taken to hospital—this would have meant closing the show, which happened in any case—therefore a doctor at a clinic prescribed morphine, to which she became addicted. Her second "dark period" had begun—the first having been the months following Marcel Cerdan's death. Incredibly it would produce some of her finest songs beginning with two

Aznavour "rejects" which he had given to Patachou and Juliette Gréco. In the meantime, there was Piaf's only song written and composed by Charles Trenet:

100: *L'âme des poètes* (The soul of poets) (Charles Trenet). October: Tape recording, archived.
Accompaniment: Robert Chauvigny & His Orchestra.
Trenet (1913-2001), one of France's most popular singer-songwriters, was known to have been an unpleasant individual. *L'âme des poètes* was his tribute to the Jewish poet Max Jacob (1876-1944), his friend and possible lover who had been arrested by the Gestapo, and who died at the Drancy internment camp while awaiting transportation to Auschwitz. Trenet performed the song in the film *Bouquet de joie*, and recorded it in January 1951—it was released whilst Piaf was appearing in *La p'tite Lili*. Why her version was archived is not known. The song, which sees Trenet changing the tense several times, was a massive hit for him, and later a hit for Juliette Gréco.

> Long after the poets have gone, their songs will run through the streets. The crowd will sing them, distracted, ignoring the author's name, unaware for whom their hearts are beating. At times they change a word, a phrase. And when they run short of ideas they go, "*La, la, la, la, la, la!*"....It's their songs that make us happy, make us sad: girls and boys, bourgeois, artists, vagabonds....One day they'll sing this tune to comfort a sorrow or some happy fate....

143

Will it help an old tramp to live, or a child to sleep? Or will it be played in spring, on a phonogram next to the water? Long after the poets are gone…

101: *Plus bleux que tes yeux* (Bluer than your eyes) (Charles Aznavour).
15 October: Columbia BF 411, A-side.
Accompaniment: Robert Chauvigny & His Orchestra.
Patachou (Henriette Ragon, 1918-2015) was an immensely popular and singer and actress. She opened the Montmartre cabaret bearing her name in 1948, and was the first artiste to cover the songs of Georges Brassens. Later in her career she took America by storm, and was also popular with British audiences. Though the first to sing *Plus bleux que tes yeux*, she did not record it until 1953:

> [Spoken]: When I raise my eyes, I see the sky and tell myself, "*My God, but it's sensational! So much blue!*" When I raise my eyes, I see your eyes and tell myself, "*It's truly wonderful, so much blue!*"
> [Sung]: I see nothing better than the blue of your eyes, not even the blue of the skies! I can't imagine anything blonder than your golden hair, not even the blond of the cornfields! Even the august wind could not be purer than your sweet breath—nothing stronger than my love for you, not even the sea in its fury! It doesn't even get close!....If you left me, my fate would change in one fell swoop [*Mon destin changerait tout à coup, du tout au tout*].

144

Next comes the downside, should their relationship end:

> Nothing, not even a rainy sky, will be greyer than the grey of my life—nothing, not even the depths of the earth, will be blacker than the black of my heart. No bottomless pit would come close to being as empty as my life, without you. Even eternity will be short, compared to the length of my heartache....It's wrong, I know well, to think about tomorrow. What's the point of complicating life when, today, I only see the dreams that your eyes bring to me?

102: *Je hais les dimanches* (I hate Sundays) (Charles Aznavour, Florence Véran)
15 October: Columbia BF 411, B-side.
4 January 1956: live, with English introduction, Carnegie Hall, New York.
Accompaniment: Robert Chauvigny & His Orchestra.
In a career spanning sixty years, Juliette Gréco (1927-2020) appeared in over thirty films, and boasted a repertoire more versatile and extensive (600+ songs recorded) than any other French female singer. Florence Véran (1922-2006) would re-enter Piaf's career towards the end of her life.

> Weekdays are empty and ring hollow. Worse than weekdays is pretentious Sunday, which wants to appear rosy and act out the generous—Sunday which imposes itself like a blessed day. I hate Sundays! In the street there's the crowd: millions of

passers-by, this crowd flowing past with an air of indifference. This crowd that walks as if at a funeral—the funeral of a Sunday that's been dead for a long time. I hate Sundays! You [her lover] work all week, and Sunday too. That's perhaps why I'm biased.

She then declares how Sundays *should* be:

Darling, if only you were close to me, I'd be ready to like everything that I dislike! Sundays in spring, flanked by the sun, brilliantly casting its rays [*qui effacent en brillant*] to erase the worries of the day before. Sundays filled with blue skies and children's laughter. Lovers' romantic strolls and timid promises. And flowers on the branches! And among the crowd, people crossing the streets without rushing. The two of us, slipping out hand-in-hand, without wanting to know what will happen tomorrow, if it will be as hopeless as other Sundays.

And ultimately, her tone becomes mocking:

And all the honest people! Those said to be well-meaning but who are not—those who *want* to be believed, who go to church because it's the custom, who change their shirts and put on nice suits! Those who sleep for twenty hours because nothing stops them from doing so. Those getting up

146

early to go fishing. Those for whom it's the day to go to the cemetery—those who make love because there's nothing else to do! [These people] would envy our happiness, just as I envy theirs—having Sundays, believing in Sundays, loving Sundays, when I *hate* Sundays!

The final song laid down in the session was a collaboration between two of Piaf's former lovers—Henri Contet and Norbert Glanzberg—who like all the others would remain on good terms with her until the end. The song, which provided Piaf with her biggest hit of the year, had a long and chequered history. Glanzberg had composed the music in 1942, when Charles Trenet had supplied the lyrics which contained the lines, "*Valsons, valsons, valsons! On oublie lorsqu'on danse la java!*" [Let's waltz, let's waltz, let's waltz! One forgets whilst dancing the java!], and presented this to Piaf who had dismissed it as "sugar-coated crap". In 1948, her former mentor Raymond Asso had come up with a lyric entitled *New York-Paris-Berlin*, which she had hated even more. Then, in the summer of 1951, Glanzberg had got together with Contet, and "the miracle", as Piaf called it, had occurred!

103: *Padam, padam* (Henri Contet, Norbert Glanzberg).
15 October: Columbia BF 429, A-side.
21 September 1952: live, *Ed Sullivan Show*. *
6 October 1952: live, Versailles, New York.
4 January 1956: with English introduction, Carnegie Hall.

Accompaniment: Robert Chauvigny & His Orchestra, with the exception of * when Piaf was accompanied by The Ed Sullivan Show Orchestra, in her US television debut.

The song was adapted into English by husband-and-wife team Mann Holiner and Alberta Nichols, retaining the title *Padam, Padam*. Vera Lynn was the first to record it—it was released by Capitol just weeks after the Piaf version—with *Auf Wiederseh'n Sweetheart* on the B-side. The following year, Columbia USA released the version by Champ Butler, with *Auf Wiederseh'n Sweetheart* on the B-side. Piaf sang it on stage in New York, but never got around to recording it in the studio. The song in its original French may almost be regarded as a companion piece to Piaf's *Je n'en connais pas la fin*, but whereas the lilting refrain of the earlier song stirs up only feelings of nostalgia and romance, the harshness of *Padam*, despite the engaging melody, suggests a hint of the fear of approaching insanity (which would resurface later in Piaf's career with songs such as *Bravo pour le clown* and *Les blouses blanches*), in this instance within the singer herself.

> This melody which obsesses me day and night didn't begin today. It goes as far back as I go back, dragged around by a hundred-thousand musicians. One day this tune will drive me insane. A hundred times, I've wanted to say why—but it cuts me off. It always speaks before I do. Its voice drowns my own. *Padam....*It comes running behind me, makes me remember, and points its finger at me, dragging

around after me like a funny mistake, this melody that knows everything [about me] by heart! It says: *"Remember your lovers! Remember, because it's your turn! There's no reason why you can't cry, with all your excess baggage!"* [encumbrance: *Avec tes souvenirs sur les bras*]. And me, I see the ones who remain. My twenties started the drum rolling. I see gestures intertwining—all the comedies of love [played out against] this melody that goes on and on for ever. *Padam*....Those Bastille Day *"I love yous"*...those *"forevers"* one buys on special offer [*qu'on achète au rabais*]. *Padam*....Those *"do you want it here?* by the packet. And all of this just to fall down at the corner of the street [on account of] the melody that recognises me! *Padam*....listen to the din that it's making! *Padam*...its as if my past is parading by! *"You must save your sorrow for later!"* I have a whole *solfège* on this melody which beats like a wooden heart!

The flipside of *Padam, padam*, a melodic but maudlin piece—this time a *double* suicide-song—earned Piaf the prestigious *Grand Prix de Deauville*, an award which, like the one she had received for *Le chevalier de Paris*, had a negative effect when she dropped it from her repertoire after singing it just twice, claiming that the excess publicity had over-commercialised it. It was recorded by Juliette Gréco and featured on the B-side of *Romance*, issued in 1952.

104: *La chanson de Catherine* (Catherine's song) (André Journiot, C. Youri, Pierre Journiot aka Pierre Damine). 8 November: Columbia BF 429, B-side.

> Here you are married, Catherine, joyless and without love. The one you love is lost forever. How sweet were the days gone by! But what's the good of mentioning them? A blackbird cries in the night: "*Yesterday, Catherine, you said 'I do!'*" Now, you must dance and forget. Why cry, beautiful child? The violins are playing tenderly.

Then comes reflection—followed by the inevitable:

> It's at the bottom of your garden—the very old oak tree where a boy had once carved your name next to his, in a single heart. Do you see, the one you loved so much? "*Beautiful blackbird, what are you telling me?*" "*He hanged himself from that oak tree!* [So] here you are married, Catherine…joyless, without love. The one you love is lost forever. Tomorrow morning little Catherine, in the frozen water of your sorrow, in the strange water of the sea, you'll float with your eyes open towards your destiny. And where the sea merges with the sky, in your satin dress you'll be reunited with your faithful lover. We see you married, Catherine—married with love! The one you love, Catherine, is forever yours!

While in America, Piaf and Charles Aznavour had attended a concert by Frankie Laine (1913-2007), in which he had introduced *Jezebel*, written by Wayne Shanklin (1916-70), whose *Chanson d'amour* would later be revived by The Manhattan Transfer. Laine was yet to record the song. Piaf met him after the show, and told him that—after hearing the song just the once—she had asked Aznavour to pen her a French adaptation. In return, she added, Laine would be "allowed" to perform a Piaf song of his choosing—but only in the original French! Piaf recorded *Jezebel* after *Padam, padam* and *La chanson de Catherine*. The recording was pressed, but held back so as not to hinder sales of the Laine recording, released in the summer. Piaf also insisted that the sides be switched around, so that *Jezebel* would be on the flipside of *La rue aux chansons*, her most uplifting song for a while. Laine waited another seven years before recording *Si tu partais*, for his *Foreign Affair* album, orchestrated by Michel Legrand. His French is beyond dire, making this arguably one of the worst ever interpretations of a Piaf song. Charles Aznavour recalled, "He sent her a copy of the recording, and she threw it in the trash!"

105: *Jezebel* (Wayne Shanklin, Charles Aznavour).
8 November: (Version 1) released posthumously.
8 November: (Version 2) Columbia BF 419, B-side.
21 September 1952: live, The Ed Sullivan Show. *
Accompaniment: Robert Chauvigny & His Orchestra, with the exception of * when Piaf was accompanied by the resident orchestra.

Piaf performs the song in the male role, and Aznavour's lyrics have nothing to do with the character in the Bible. Version 1, which Piaf asked to be archived, runs at 3:30 and has a full choir backing throughout. Version 2 has just the choral introduction.

> Jezebel! Jezebel! The demon who burned my heart, the angel who dried my tears, those tears impaled with joy—it's you, Jezebel! But love destroyed itself. Everything in my life has tumbled down—crushing, trampling, taking my life away. But for you, Jezebel, I would make a trip around the world. I would go to the bowels of hell [*j'irais jusqu'au fond des enfers*]. Where are you, Jezebel? Where are you? The memories we believed to be faded are living things with eyes of death, still vibrating in the past. But my heart is punctured with obsession. It beats deep inside me, repeating the word that I love—your name, Jezebel!....I would make a trip around the world. I would go to the bowels of hell, shouting relentlessly, day and night: "*Jezebel!*"

106: *La rue aux chansons* (Street of songs) (Michel Emer). 8 November: BF 419, A-side.
Accompaniment: Robert Chauvigny & His Orchestra. Choir: Raymond Saint-Paul.

It's the street of songs, the street of joy, where in all

the houses, without rhyme or reason, we're singing out loud! Since daybreak, everyone is happy, and in the grey suburbs each one in turn invents a blue sky. There, we don't come across unhappy lovers. They love, don't love, kiss and go on their way. They're singing, and there you are! You, the disenchanted ones who weep for no reason—to learn how to sing, go and live in the street of songs! We'll hug each other a little. There is for three [lovers] what there [usually] is for two. We don't care about luxury and comfort. No need for that in the rue de Cigale! It's the street of song, the street of joy…

Piaf rounded off this year with two visits to the studio—and two on-stage recording sessions on stage in an empty Théâtre des Champs-Elysées for reasons which have never been explained—to record four very different songs, only one of which would be performed on the stage. Unlike most entertainers, she had always steered clear of seasonal songs, believing that good songs should be performed all year round and not limited to a specific season. She had performed *Il est né le divin* enfant in America but never in France, and in 1949 had declined to join Les Compagnons de la Chanson for their recording of *Douce nuit*. Now, she asked Henri Contet to write her a "suitable" Christmas song—and of course, it had to be dramatic.

107: *C'est toi* (It's you) (Edith Piaf, Robert Chauvigny). 23 November: Columbia BF 464, A-side.

Accompaniment: Robert Chauvigny & His Orchestra.
Solo version of the song from *La p'tite Lili*, recorded at the Théâtre des Champs-Elysées. In this version, there is no interlude in English.

108: *Le Noël de la rue* (The Christmas of the street) (Henri Contet, Marc Heyral).
23 November: Columbia BF 464, B-side.
Accompaniment: Robert Chauvigny & His Orchestra. Choir: Raymond Saint-Paul.
The song comprises mostly of a conversation between a poor woman and a street urchin, enviously gazing at the contents of a shop window.

> WOMAN: *Little fellow, where are you going, running around barefoot, like this?*
> BOY: *I'm running after heaven—for it's Christmas, they say! Christmas in the streets is the snow and the wind, and the wind in the streets makes the children cry!*
> WOMAN: Light and joy are behind the shop windows, not for you or me [but] for our neighbour. My little one, amuse yourself looking, but above all, touch nothing while looking from afar!"
> NARRATOR: The Christmas of the streets is the winter's cold in the wide open eyes of the street children. Their snouts glued to the shop windows, all the little ones curve their backs, huddled [against the cold] like the little Jesus, whom the Virgin Mary

would have lost [a reference to the *pieta*]. The Christmas of the street is the snow and the wind, and the wind of the street makes the children cry. They go on their way sniffling, empty-handed, their noses in the air looking for the splendid star.

WOMAN: Little one, if you see it whilst walking, warm your little hands on it whilst walking upright!

NARRATOR: The Christmas of the street is the heaven of their life—a sleeping star which has not descended.

109: *À l'enseigne de la Fille Sans Coeur* (The sign of The Heartless Girl) (Gilles).

23 November: Columbia BF 436, A-side.

Accompaniment: Robert Chauvigny & His Orchestra. Choir: Raymond Saint-Paul.

Written by Jean Villard, who had formerly provided Piaf with *Les trois cloches*, under his more familiar pseudonym. The song had been presented to Piaf in 1947, but put aside until now. *La Fille Sans Coeur* is the dockside brothel where the sailors take refuge when their ship, bound for America, is blown off-course during a storm and runs aground, and also the name they award the boss's daughter, undeservedly so because, unlike the other girls, she is not a prostitute. Much of the song is also written in *argot*, and therefore may only be paraphrased.

The sky is blue, the strong wind hollows out the sea. The troupe head towards the port, at the edge of the

155

world, where the streets lead nowhere—as sure as the world is round, they don't see the United States! Nobody gives a damn. There's happiness at The Heartless Girl—a bar run by Rita the Blonde! * The accordion plays full-blast, tunes from around the world. There's Rita with her kiss-curls….She reigns in this little bar. They see her golden mane, her mouth like a bleeding fruit, but they say her heart is dead. Yet the boys are there: little ones, tough ones, Malabars [an ethnic group of Tamil origin from Réunion], and there are some men come here from Dakar who walk in, swaggering their shoulders. There are men from Antwerp and Honfleur, backpacking on their way to the Pole. They look at [the girl]. She makes them happy, but not one of them has known her favours. The accordion plays full-blast—all the melodies, sad and funny. There are men who stake out their happiness [pay for prostitutes] at The Heartless Girl. The boss knew his stuff [*le patron connaissait la musique*]. He liked the sound of coins. He said to his only daughter, "*Avoid love—it's a waste of time!*"

For the girl however there is a surprise, when her estranged lover turns up. None of the others have seen him before, and until now he seems to have been unaware that she is living here:

One evening, the sea raged and in walked a stranger

156

with eyes as blue as a cloudless sky [rough translation: *aux beaux yeux d'azur sans nuages*]. That's when everything changed. He looked at the heartless girl. Her reaction was feisty [*elle était comme un ciel d'orage*] and someone said, "*Here's trouble!*" Then we heard hearts beating. The accordion played a melody—*The Wild Wind*—in low-key, and there's a girl, tears streaming down her face, at The Heartless Girl. ** He said, "*It's you, divine lady!*" She said, "*Yes, I'm yours!*" He held her to his breast—she wept in his arms. Then the others, feeling melancholy, sighed and left. The wind sang over the Atlantic for the heart that had just opened. They [the lovers] rushed off to celebrate their great happiness [rough translation: *ils ont filé vers leur grand bonheur*], and the boss had to shut up shop. He was seen drinking all his liquors at The Heartless Girl.

The ending little sense with direct translation: [*L'accordéon accapareur, qu'a jamais eu l'sens du comique/ A mis le bureau du Percepteur/ À l'enseigne de la Fille Sans Coeur* = The hoarding accordion, who never had a sense of comedy / Has put the tax collector's office / In the name of the Heartless Girl]. One therefore *may* assume that Rita drank all the profits, and became bankrupt!

* One is given the impression that Rita is a drag-queen, as Gilles uses the term *le patron*, and not *la patronne*, and alternates between calling the character *he* and *she*.

** Here, Gilles is referring to *Le vent m'a dit une chanson,* a song popularised by Damia.

110: *Télégramme* (Telegram) (Michel Emer).
25 November: Columbia BF 436, B-side. *
Accompaniment: Robert Chauvigny & His Orchestra.
13 January 1957: live at Carnegie Hall, New York, with English introduction.
 * as **#107**, recorded at the Théâtre des Champs-Elysées.

The story of the lovers forced apart when young because she was rich, and he poor. Now his fortune has changed, and a reunion arranged—save that what he has not counted on is that they have aged, and no longer look as they did. It begins with the postman speaking to the concierge:

> *"This is a telegram for Marie Bélage!"*
> *"In the courtyard—Staircase B, 5th floor, third door on the left, then you descend two steps. Knock loudly so that she can hear you..."*
> The little postman climbs the steps four at a time. An old maid comes to open the door.* In a harsh, cantankerous voice she tells him, "Thank you!" and then goes back in. Trembling, she opens the dispatch. Generally, she doesn't like these things. Her throat dry, she reads aloud, then lowers her voice and reads it ten times more: *I'll be at Orly—2 May—8 am—I'm impatient—Overjoyed—I adore you more than ever—Love—Kisses—François!*

158

She goes back twenty years. How they were in love! But her parents wouldn't accept him. He didn't have a penny. He told her, *"I'll come back when I've made my fortune!"* She told him, *"I'll wait for you. I also want you to promise never to forget me!"* He left. Months and years pass. She's all alone in life. Beauty, freshness, youth—they all disappear. And more money, therefore more friends...

Then comes the confusion at the airport, when he brushes past her, not recognising her, and she tears up the telegram:

The passengers arrive from Mexico. *"Here he is! How tall he is!"* His greying temples give him a poetic air. He's more handsome than he was twenty years ago. She's very pale and her hands are burning. How her poor heart beats so! He walks towards her, only to jostle past. He asks: *"Excuse me, porter. I'm looking for an elegant lady—very beautiful, big blue eyes, blonde hair, rather small! Wait—I think that's her! No, that's not her! Sorry!"*

Thus he ambles around the lounge, repeating the same question, in vain: Has anyone seen a blond, elegant and very beautiful lady?

*Critics at the time posed: if the woman had been so young to have required her parents' permission then why, twenty years on, was she being referred to as "an old maid"?

111: *Tous mes rêves passes* (All my past dreams) (Edith Piaf, Marguerite Monnot).

December: Solo recording, archived.

8 September 1952: Columbia BF 496, A-side, sung by Jacques Pills.

This song was written for Eddie Constantine, but when they split up she gave the song to Lucienne Delyle. Constantine recorded it, regardless (Columbia BF 390, B-side), and even "purloined" Piaf's musicians. Accompaniment (all three versions): Robert Chauvigny & His Orchestra.

All my past dreams are far behind me. I see before me our tears to come. What has become of you, blue flower of my faded twenties? What do you want? My dreams are too big. And you (meaning herself) wise-hearted girl! How pure were your eyes! What, along the way, has made you impure? All my past dreams are far behind me, but reality walks ahead of me. I see myself again when I was twenty, all the sorrows I must have caused my mother—lost hopes carried off by the wind, and now I have no more ambition. I've used up all my illusions, (but) I've returned rich with memories. Memories can always be useful! All my past dreams are far behind me...my dreams are too big. And when I'm going along my way and a twenty-year old boy passes by, I see my face again and smile sadly. Just as a tune lingers for a long time, I cling to my sorrows, my dreams when I was twenty.

160

La p'tite Lili.

With Robert Lamoureux and Patachou.

1952

In the spring of this year, Raymond Asso (1901-68) re-entered Piaf's life, but briefly, to offer her a song. They had been lovers before World War Two when she had been starting her career, a relationship which had proved volatile but productive. Her first big successes—*Mon legionnaire, Le fanion de la Légion* and *Je n'en connais pas la fin*, to mention but three—had been penned by him. Had Asso offered her *more* than a song—himself—she might have avoided the disasters and pitfalls of the years to come, for only he would have been strong enough to control or even put a stop to her drug-taking and increasing dependency on the bottle. Asso was engaged to be married to the actress Claude Valéry (1909-92), who set his poem to music—the first song that Piaf recorded this year, earmarked as the A-side of her next release. The setting, pretty much like *Le prisonnier de la Tour* and recalling Asso's earlier *Un jeune homme chantait* (Volume 1, **#31**) is in medieval France, but unlike these two does not make much sense. Curiously, though the orchestration and Piaf's voice are exquisite, the lyric does not have an ending, leaving the listener guessing as to what happens next.

112: *Mon ami m'a donné* (My friend gave me). (Raymond Asso, Claude Valéry).
28 June: Columbia 33 FS 1014 (10-inch vinyl album).
Accompaniment: Robert Chauvigny & His Orchestra.
Harpist: unknown.

My friend gave me a flower which I put to my heart—on my heart full of him. How that rose was beautiful, how my heart was full of him! Happiness bloomed! My friend gave me a kiss, sweetly placed next to my love-filled heart. How his lips were sweet—that kiss I gave in return filled with love! My friend gave me an oath to love me for a long time, as long as flowers will grow on earth, as long as his flower stays on my heart. My friend made me cry, crying that I didn't deserve. I took the white rose to dry my tears—the rose that was on my heart. My friend will come to see me tomorrow, more flowers and much sorrow. I'll go and steal flowers from the world's gardens—the most beautiful in my heart. If they want to throw me in prison, I'll tell those who judge me, "Beat the drums and get the gallows ready! Rather than lose love, I'll flee France! And the King in his court, rather than losing love…"

The next man in Piaf's life put paid to the Asso song being released as her next 78 rpm single, resulting in it being relegated to Piaf's first vinyl album release in France. Jacques Pills (René Ducos, 1906-70) is claimed by many to have been her greatest mistake. He had achieved fame in the 1930s as one half of Pills & Tabet, with Georges Tabet (1905-84). Their biggest success had been *Couchés dans le foin*, in 1932, but by 1952 their kind of harmonising had gone out of fashion.

Everyone that I interviewed about Pills had the same opinion of him—that he had been an opportunist. Marlene Dietrich recalled:

> Edith needed an iron hand to guide her back on to the rails, a man who genuinely cared about her, and not for what he was getting out of her. Pills knew his career was over but he hung on because of the money. Afterwards, Edith told me she had told him she was taking drugs on account of her rheumatism, and that he had believed her. Now, that man was anything but stupid. He knew what she was doing, and he did nothing to stop her because his own career was finished and she was paying for everything. I told her, "Get rid of that son-of-a-bitch and find yourself a real husband!"

Pills had embarked on a relationship with Joséphine Baker in 1933. In 1939, he had married Lucienne Boyer, and they had divorced in 1951. He was involved with Joséphine for a second time when Piaf proposed to *him*—she joking that it *was* a leap year—and it was reported at the time that before giving her his response he had called Joséphine, working in New York, with the ultimatum, "Marry me, or I'll marry Piaf!" He also lied about his age, knocking off seven years. Joséphine's assistant at the time—Gracie Fields' stepdaughter Irene Bevan, remembered:

> Jacques Pills' thing was preying on famous women.

165

He [the first time around] used Joséphine like a stepping-stone, then dropped her like a hot brick once his own career got under way. Her every move was vetted by him. He handled her bookings and contracts, and her money, much of which went into his own pocket. When he finally married Lucienne Boyer, he went around boasting that theirs was a marriage made in heaven, yet he was never faithful to her and it ended in divorce. It's easy to understand how such a charlatan could have pulled the wool over Piaf's eyes. Like Joséphine she was astonishingly naïve where men were concerned, though by the time she got around to him she'd had more than her share of men and she should have known better. Thankfully, when she realized what kind of man he was, she dropped *him* like a hot brick.

Like so many of his predecessors, Pills charmed his way into Piaf's affections by bringing her a song which he had written with his pianist, Gilbert Silly (1927-2001) who became Gilbert Bécaud. Raymond Asso was furious with her for dropping his song for one which he considered inferior—which lyrically it was—and vowed never to write for her again. He stuck to his word, though she would seek him out towards the end of her life.

113: *Je t'ai dans la peau* (I've got you under my skin) (Jacques Pills, Gilbert Bécaud).

166

May: live recording, Radio France.
Piano accompaniment: Robert Chauvigny.
28 June: Columbia BF 491, A-side.
July: soundtrack recording for the film, *Boum sur Paris!*
4 January 1956: French and English, Carnegie Hall.
Accompaniment: Robert Chauvigny & His Orchestra.

With the exception of *Dany* (**#55**), the most suggestive song that Piaf ever performed. Nothing was said when she first sang a muted version of this live on the radio, but there were so many complaints from listeners when the recording was aired—whilst the Catholic Church declared it immoral because of "the heavy breathing and sexual groaning". Thus it was banned from the airwaves, which only added to its popularity. It would remain a highlight of Piaf's recitals until 1958, by which time she would have divorced Jacques Pills—though some audience members objected to the way she ran her hands seductively up and down her body, pretending that these were the hands of her lover (as also happens in the film) whilst singing it.

> You, always you, nothing but you, everywhere you! I've got you under my skin. There's nothing to be done. Stubbornly, you're there! I try to rid myself of it. You're always close to me....all over my body. I'm cold, I'm hot, I feel the fever on my skin. I don't give a damn what people might think. I can't stop shouting. You're everything for me. I'm intoxicated. I love you to death! I've got you under my skin! There's nothing to be done…

Lyrically and melody-wise, the B-side of *Je t'ai dans la peau* was far superior, and because of the ban imposed on the A-side, this was the song that received all the airplay, though Piaf curiously never sang it on stage. She *did* use the title, several years later, for her first autobiography, the script of which was also censored in parts—particularly when discussing her early years—so as not to offend more sensitive readers.

114: *Au bal de la chance* (At the lucky ball) (Jacques Larue, Norbert Glanzberg).
28 June: Columbia BF 491, B-side.
Accompaniment: Robert Chauvigny & His Orchestra.
The girl in the song, of course, is Piaf herself.

> All along the grass verge, the water flows and bubbles. The superb sky dazzles the surroundings. The big sun plays *boules* with the blossoming apple trees. The ball, in front of the flowing water, rehashes Parisian tunes. Dance—dance at the lucky ball! Dance, my daydreams! With slow gestures, the parasols on the river-bank take a bow to the barges, while a girl dances in the arms of a sailor. The sky is reckless, but this love is not her last. Dance at the ball of chance, in the spring sky! The wind, turning in the groves makes bouquets with the song of the finches, but she hardly listens. And how the boy's such vulgar words make the finches laugh in the sky! Dance at the ball of chance....dance with my song! I think once more about that day last year. My

dream is imprisoned on my shoulder, neither one thing nor the other [*cela n'a ni queue ni tête*]. Therefore I have a very heavy heart—for sailors on leave, love is always renewing. Love—*that* flows over the water! Dance, dance at the ball of chance! Dance, my birdlike heart!

Part of the summer was taken up with the shooting of *Boum sur Paris!* The storyline was poor: a flask of perfume containing an explosive has been hidden amongst the prizes at a raffle and is known to have been won by an entertainer. The police go looking for it, and in the process we get to hear some of the greatest French singers of the day.

The civil ceremony for Piaf and Pills took place on 29 July 1952, whilst their "real" wedding took place in New York on 20 September, in the middle of her American tour. The witnesses were her manager Louis Barrier and Marlene Dietrich, who despite her closeness to Piaf took a great deal of persuading, as she recalled:

> The first time I met Jacques Pills, I took an immediate dislike to him. That man was too charming for his own good, and it was all put on. Because she pleaded with me, because I loved her so very much, I gave in. That day I kept looking at her, hoping she would be capable of staying on her feet. She was very happy, but very sick. I remember saying to myself, "I hope this is going to work out for her," though I knew that it never would.

169

115: *Ça gueule ça, Madame* (Madame's bawling) (Edith Piaf, Gilbert Bécaud)
July: soundtrack recording for the film, *Boum sur Paris!*
8 September: Columbia BF 496, A-side.
3 April 1954: live on TV, *La joie de vivre d'Edith Piaf.*
Accompaniment: Robert Chauvigny & His Orchestra.
Piaf's first of three collaborations with Gilbert Bécaud. Performed by Jacques Pills, with Piaf coming in only on the closing line. The song, which tells of the infamous Piaf temper recalled and feared by so many who knew her, may be better understood by watching Pills' gestures in the film, or in the television show.

> PILLS: She's this high. No, I exaggerate. Like this...or more like this. She might not look much—but for goodness sake she takes up space, this bit of nothing!* And Madame's bawling! You only hear her in the house! She puts on quite a show! If there are none, she looked for reasons to yell. With her, everything's a drama....She yells at the top of her voice, *"Don't think you frighten me!"* She's tense. She stamps her foot—unsheathes her claws, opens her eyes, gets furious. I want to take her in my arms and hold her close to me. But Madame's bawling! It makes me laugh, but foremost and deep inside I'm a gentleman, and it's wiser to calm her down so I try and think of a way [rough translation: *je cherche un truc*]. I tell myself, *"Let's see—I'll give her credit!"* And I tell her, *"It's*

me who's wrong!" "Oh, you admit it!" she says.
And Madame starts bawling again! And even when
things are going swimmingly [rough translation:
même que tout valse] at home, she's looking for
reasons to make a whole drama out of *that*!
Madame's bawling—it gets me right here in the
heart! So once, to frighten her, I clenched my fists. I
raised my hand. She looked so surprised—if you
saw her eyes, you'd think she'd been punished! She
flung herself against me—and Madame's weeping!
I search everywhere for a big handkerchief to hide
her despair which was painful to see. I consoled her
and blew her nose, and a little later kissed her on the
mouth. I held her against me and enclosed her in my
arms. She's so small…so very small! For a little
while that meant sorry. But Madame's not proud!
Even so, there was satisfaction in making her admit
that she was wrong, and that I'm the stronger one!

In the film—and when he performed the song on *La joie de
vivre d'Edith Piaf*—Pills is smug and pleased with himself
that he has put his wife in her place, until he looks at his
watch and says, *"Oh, my God, I'm late! Madame's going to
start yelling!"*—bringing a shout from Piaf, *"Jacques, are
you coming?"* before she stomps on to drag him off.

* In the song, the expression used is *nom d'un chien*, used
as an alternative to *nom de Dieu* (for God's sake) so as not
to blaspheme.

116: *Pour qu'elle soit jolie ma chanson* (To make my song beautiful) (Edith Piaf, Louiguy).

July: longer version, soundtrack recording for the film, *Boum sur Paris!*

15 July 1953: BF 589, B-side.

Accompaniment: Robert Chauvigny & His Orchestra.

A duet with Jacques Pills, where they juxtapose the lyrics with those of some of Piaf's hits, notably *La vie en rose*, along with those of *Ça gueule ça, Madame* ,though *Bravo pour le clown* was yet to be recorded.

> PILLS: There are songs that are hits because the music is very popular.
>
> PIAF: *Quand il me prend dans ses bras.* Something like that?
>
> PILLS: Yes, that's not bad. There are songs that are big hits because the words are out of the ordinary.
>
> PIAF: *Et ça gueule ça, Madame!*
>
> PILLS: Hey—I heard that one somewhere! There are songs that are big hits because the performer is *extra*ordinary.
>
> PIAF: That's almost always so!
>
> PILLS: But my (song) doesn't have all that. I'm going to tell you why. To make my song beautiful, first of all there must be two—a boy, of course, and a girl to make him happy. If you'll loan me your voice to sing this love song with me? There's nothing original about it. It's normal that *amour* (love) rhymes with *toujours* (always).*

172

PIAF: I'm sorry, but the song lacks that special something. So you can tell the boy that this song's not for me!

PILLS: I can see what you need. A port and a sailor, bar-room brawls, nothing but sinister things. A poor man getting hanged, people talking loud. A distinguished gentleman, an accordionist. I've even heard—and that's *too* fanciful!—that you sang about a clown! Well, bravo for the clown! No—no, come on! You're yelling at me! Oh, pardon me—I got a little carried away, there!

PIAF: So, in your opinion, will this song be for me? Well, listen. Sing it to me again!

PILLS: To make my song beautiful...

BOTH: First of all there must be two.

PILLS: And of course, a boy...

BOTH: And a girl to make him happy! So, lend me your voice to sing this love song with me. There's nothing original about it. All in all, it's not bad that *amour* rhymes with *toujours*.

PIAF: My song's so lovely, for I'm singing it despite of me [this not being her usual genre of song]. So you can tell the boy that this song is good for me!

---

* A long-standing demand that Piaf made of her lyricists was that *amour* should never rhyme with *toujours*, because this common practice was as a result of lack of sensible thinking. In an interview she said this was the equivalent of

173

some American lyricists rhyming *moon* with *June*, because they lacked the talent to come up with anything better!

Piaf's American tour opened as usual at the Versailles, in New York, where Pills joined her on stage to sing the two duets from *Boum sur Paris!* The pair appeared on several television shows, and after one, Piaf was introduced to the lyricist Carl Sigman (1909-2000), who later in his career would adapt many Continental songs into English. Sigman had heard Eddie Constantine singing *Tous mes rêves passés*, and adapted this into English. Piaf performed this during the tour, but never got around to recording it, so far as is known. It became a hit for Dinah Shore.

117: *Why Come Crying To Me?* (Edith Piaf, Carl Sigman). September: NBC Television, New York.
The English-language adaptation of *Tous mes rêves passés*. Like some of Piaf's earlier songs adapted into English, notably *C'est de la faute* and *Je m'en fous pas mal*, the lyrics have nothing to do with the French originals.

Upon Piaf's return to Paris, there were two visits to the studio. Three of the six songs were archived: and another was released posthumously, whilst the remaining two have yet to resurface. The first song laid down in the session, earmarked for release, was archived upon Piaf's insistence when she learned that it had already been recorded by Lucienne Delyle. It is a beautiful song, but lyrically does not always make sense.

118: *Notre Dame de Paris* (Marc Heyral, Eddy Marnay).

3 September: USA Columbia Masterworks A-1812, 7-inch vinyl, released posthumously.

Accompaniment: Robert Chauvigny & His Orchestra.

Eddy Marnay (1920-2003) wrote over 4,000 songs, and there are few French singers who have *not* performed one of his compositions. He had provided the lyrics for Piaf's earlier *Les amants de Paris*, and would work with her again. His other hits included Frida Boccara's 1969 joint Eurovision winner *Un jour un enfant*, his adaptation for her of *The Windmills of Your Mind* (*Les moulins de mon coeur*), and his adaptation of *The Shadow of Your Smile* (*Le sourire de mon amour*) for Juliette Gréco.

In the Paris of Notre Dame, from Notre Dame of Paris there's a tramp carrying Notre Dame on his back. People think he's Quasimodo! Instead of making circles in the water, look up into the air—life teems! You cannot live like a frog, half on earth, half in the water! Me, I prefer staying up there in the garden of Notre Dame where we make good friends. You only have to walk each morning, a little maize in the palm of your hand. Me, I like the pigeons very much. The barges don't care for the pigeons of the city. Schooners dislike [aka: *elles n'ont que ça dans l'idée*] seagulls. But around Notre Dame there are cheap boat-trips [*bateaux mouches*]. And little corners of happiness prevent the houses from growing. It's called the Flower Market! Henry

IV. Greenery. Love under the grey grass. The Flèche (the medieval timber spire, destroyed in the fire of April 2019) which licks the grey ceiling of Paris. And you, under the bridge of Notre Dame!* Look up into the air! You'll understand that if everyone was in your drunken state, it would rain! Even the bridges are built! For to go to Notre Dame, from Notre Dame back to Paris, he had to get to work and carry stones on his back and cross over the water. That's why Paris rolls along like a snail—why the earth gets into a ball around the bells in the courtyard of Notre Dame of Paris! **

*Here, Marnay is referring to the tramps living under the bridges of the Île de la Cité, and ** to the Île itself.

119: *L'an deux-milles* (The year 2,000) (René Rouzaud, Marguerite Monnot).
3 September: archived.
Accompaniment: Robert Chauvigny & His Orchestra).
This song is listed in the archives of Editions Salabert as having been recorded and performed on stage. There are no further details. It was the first song written for Piaf by René Rouzaud (1905-75), who went on to have many subsequent triumphs not just with Piaf, but with many other greats of the *chanson.*

120: *Hymne à la jeunesse* (Hymn to youth) (Gilbert Bécaud, Edith Piaf).

3 September: archived.

Accompaniment: Robert Chauvigny & His Orchestra.

The second of the three collaborations between Piaf and Bécaud. No other details.

121: *Elle a dit* (She said) (Gilbert Bécaud, Edith Piaf.

3 September: archived, released 1966 on the vinyl album, *Mes premières chansons: Vol. 27*, Columbia CTX 40367.

The third and final Piaf-Bécaud collaboration this year (they collaborated again three years later)—and another favourite theme—suicide. We get to hear what the lovers said on either side of their split whilst the narrator, aka Piaf, expresses her philosophies, though in this one the listener is left guessing exactly *how* the spurned party ends it all.

Accompaniment: Robert Chauvigny & His Orchestra.

Choir: Raymond Saint-Paul.

She said, *"You know we two are finished? What's the point of hanging onto each other?"*

You have to learn how to keep your dignity—and in any case, I don't like to see a man cry.

"It's best that we part as good friends. Understand—help me, and smile!"

Thus he did as she asked. Before her, as he left, he was singing: *"La, la, la..."*....When he was sleeping alone in his double-bed, he suddenly understood that this would be harder than he'd thought. And alone in his bed, he wept....

He said, *"I can't believe that it's over. I feel like I'm*

going to hang on..."

It's beautiful, keeping one's dignity—but it does you so much good to cry!

"*When I think of the day that's about to break—the things I'll have to hide—I don't think I'll ever get used to it...*"

To end it all with dignity, he…

Piaf starts to sing, "*Il s'est suicidé*" (He committed suicide) but does not finish the phrase as the music and choir drown her voice. She then concludes:

All alone, he weeps in eternity.

Piaf's final recording this year came about as a result of Michel Emer being given an explicit instruction. A month before her wedding, he was asked to supply her with two songs, the subject of both being wedding anniversaries. One would depict how happy she was expecting she and Pills would be in twenty years' time—which given both of their track-records seemed unlikely. The other, she said, would end with one of the wife planning a romantic celebration, only to learn at the last minute that her husband had been killed in a road accident! For now, she chose the former, though like *Mon ami m'a donné* she asked for it not to be released just yet—as her clairvoyant had informed her that her marriage might not last if she boasted about her happiness *before* her wedding!

122: *Monsieur et Madame* (Michel Emer)
8 September: Columbia 33 FS 1014 (10-inch vinyl album)
Accompaniment: Robert Chauvigny & His Orchestra.

Monsieur and Madame have returned from a trip. They've celebrated their 20th wedding anniversary. He takes his pyjamas from his luggage while she puts some grease on her face. Monsieur gets into bed, closes his eyes, yawns wide. *"Goodnight, darling!"* Madame puts out the light. "Move up a little!" She stretches out next to him. But in the darkness, he doesn't sleep. He goes back in time. He dreams of the blue-eyed girl, of her sensual mouth. He thinks about her wonderful body—her hands so small and beautiful. He hears her voice and her laughter and heaves an unhappy sigh. Monsieur doesn't sleep, and stretches out. He dreams of the blue-eyed girl! Madame, likewise in her little corner, is far away and doesn't sleep. She dreams of the blue-eyed boy—of his sensual mouth. Those hands, so strong and beautiful! Monsieur takes Madame in his arms. They both close their eyes, whisper *"I love you!"* to each other, and live a wonderful dream! Monsieur and Madame are happy! There are some curious relationships!

180

11 June: receiving the *Grand Prix du Disque*
from politician Edouard Herriot and Colette.

Piaf and Pills cut their wedding cake,
while Marlene looks on.

1953

In the spring of 1953, Piaf and Pills rented a new apartment at 67bis boulevard Lannes, an opulent quarter overlooking the Bois de Boulogne, which would remain her home for the remainder of her life. All the time he lived here, *she* would pay the bills. Their union was doomed from the start. No man had ever been able to control her, and Pills was too weak to try and do so now. In an attempt to hang on to him, she demanded that theatres have them both on the same bill, which few were willing to do, deeming that Pills had had his day. She therefore opted to revive *Le bel indifferent*, with Pills in the role of Emile. This would take up the first half of the bill while the second half would have Piaf and Pills singing duets—of her songs! She lavished a fortune of her own money on the project, even importing two mandolinists from Italy—though these were put to good use during her first visit to the studio this year.

123: *Les amants de Venise* (The lovers of Venice) (Jacques Plante, Marguerite Monnot).
23 May: Version 1: Columbia BF 567, B-side.
28 May: Version 2: released posthumously.
Accompaniment: Robert Chauvigny & His Orchestra.
The song, operatic in composition, tells of two young Romany lovers, compelled to live on the outskirts of Paris, who imagine they are in Venice, where the dirty gutters are transformed into streams. In Version 2, Piaf sings "*la-la-la*" over the closing music.

She told him, *"We could believe we're in Venice, where the streams are overflowing with grey water!"* How it was raining! She told him, *"We could believe we're in a gondola—I hear your heart playing its barcarole!"* How it was raining! There they were, huddled together in their gypsy caravan, with the night and a storm at the door....He replied, *"But we are in Venice!"* How they loved each other! *"Here are the lights, twinkling by the hundred—the lovely night streaked with lanterns. Close your eyes. You'll see it better!"* But all they saw was a paltry streetlamp which didn't even illuminate their misery. And over there at the corner of the street, a little blue plaque upon which they saw written, "Porte d'Italie".

Rehearsals for *Le bel indifférent* had begun in April, but had stopped when Piaf had entered a detoxification clinic to cure her of her morphine addiction which had become progressively worse in the wake of her 1951 car accident. Because the major Parisian theatres were reluctant to risk her falling ill, resulting in cancellations, she funded the project herself and hired the Théâtre Marigny—and to direct, Raymond Rouleau, who had been at the helm of *La p'tite Lili*. In the meantime, the entire piece was recorded in the studio. "Le bel indifférent" is her on-stage lover, first played (in 1940) by her then real-life lover, Paul Meurisse, and who does not utter one word, preferring to lounge on the bed reading his newspaper while she rants and raves.

124: *Le bel indifférent* (The handsome indifferent man).
A one-act play by Jean Cocteau.
Song (the recording): *Je t'ai dans la peau.*
28 May: Columbia: FS 1021 (10-inch vinyl album).

The production was a flop. The critics hammered Piaf, and audiences booed Pills, who proved hopeless in the play, even in a silent role. To cope, Piaf began drinking heavily, and against her manager's advice embarked on a tour of the provinces where several times *she* was booed for forgetting the lines of her songs. Her studio work, on the other hand, was its usual perfection. Observing how she was enduring a martyrdom some evening on stage, Gilbert Bécaud penned her a song *about* suffering. She finally recorded Michel Emer's second "wedding anniversary" song—and there was a new version of *Hymne à l'amour.*

125: *Les croix* (The crosses) (Gilbert Bécaud, Louis Amade).
15 July: Columbia BF 589, A-side.
Accompaniment: Robert Chauvigny & His Orchestra.
Choir: Raymond Saint-Paul. Solo soprano unknown.
Louis Amade (1915-92). Cabinet minister, poet and man of letters, Bécaud's mentor who worked with him often. One of their best known collaborations is *L'important c'est la rose. Les croix* was reprised by Damia, who sang it on *La joie de vivre d'Edith Piaf,* in 1956—the great singer's swansong. Note that in beginning each section with the words "*Mon Dieu*", Piaf is not blaspheming, but praying.

My God, there are some crosses on this earth! Iron crosses, wooden crosses, humble family crosses. Little silver crosses dangling on chests, old convent crosses lost among the ruins. And me—poor me—I have my cross inside my head, an immense leaden cross, vast as love. I press on against the wind. I hold back the storm. I prolong the day and hide the night within the cross inside my head. One word is engraved upon it that resembles *souffrir* (to suffer). But this familiar word that my lips repeat is so hard to carry. I think it's *mourir* (to die)! My God, there are silent crosses watching over the world on deep (aka country) roads. High-up crosses of forgiveness pointing towards the gallows (of long ago)—unreasonable crosses, or of deliverance. But me—poor me—I have the immense leaden cross inside my head....so heavy to carry, that I think of dying!

126: *Jean et Martine* (Michel Emer).
15 July: Columbia BF 589, B-side.
Accompaniment: Robert Chauvigny & His Orchestra.

Long-distance lorry driver Jean rolls along the highway. There are trees and fields. The rain is pouring down [*à grosses gouttes*]. There are sharp bends in the road. There's wind—the cold and the sunshine. There's day—night, fatigue, sleep. And the fifteen tonnes (his lorry) makes a lot of noise...

185

And at their house there's also his little Martine, and her song. "*Jean's coming home from his round*," Martine sings in her kitchen. "*He's sure to be tired. He'll be worn out, but I'll be able to look at him—to kiss him while he's eating his dinner—to look after him, cuddle him and hold myself against his breast. Later, when he's asleep, I'll be the one in his arms!*"

And this being a typical Piaf-Emer "*Find me a new way to die*" drama, things inevitably go wrong, leaving her grief-stricken...

There's fog at her window. Martine is waiting...The doorbell rings. It's a man with a letter. He seems gloomy, annoyed. "*The company...condolences...an accident...sign here. There's the funeral arrangements...the insurance policy!*" Martine, however, doesn't understand. It's not true—she doesn't believe him! [She sings, before breaking down]: "*Jean's coming home from his round....He's sure to be tired....I'll hold myself against his breast! Later, when he's sleeping...No! No! Oh, Jean!*"

Piaf had admired British singer Dorothy Squires (1915-98) for some time. In 1946, she had asked Marc Lanjean (1903-64) to adapt two of her songs—*I'll Close My Eyes* and *The Gypsy*, both by Billy Reid—into French. Lanjean only adapted the latter, and Piaf gave this to her lover at the

186

time, Yvon Jean-Claude. Dorothy recalled her association with Piaf, which happened early in 1953:

> I was working the cabaret circuit in Hollywood, and one evening I introduced *If You Love Me*, Really Love Me, the new English version of *Hymne à l'amour*. I'd met Piaf briefly at a party a few weeks earlier, and had no idea that she was in the audience. When she walked into my dressing room I was terrified—even more so when she told me that she didn't care for my arrangement of her song. Then, before I could offer my excuses she said, in broken English, "But you've got a lovely voice. Don't worry, I'll write an arrangement for you myself!" And that's exactly what she did.

Until now, Piaf had been singing Eddie Constantine's English adaptation of the song for American audiences, but this was now dropped in favour of the new version.

127: *If You Love Me, Really Love Me* (Geoffrey Parsons, Edith Piaf, Marguerite Monnot).
15 July: archived.
13 November 1955: live, *The Ed Sullivan Show*, New York.
4 January 1956: live, Carnegie Hall, New York.
Accompaniment: Robert Chauvigny & His Orchestra.
Dorothy Squires was the first to record the song, later in the year for the US market, whilst Vera Lynn released a cover version in Britain.

The day after this recording session, Piaf announced that she and Pills would be augmenting this year's Super-Circus tour—a gruelling schedule of 90 venues. Henri Contet and Louiguy were given twenty-four hours to come up with a song—about a clown—with which Piaf would close each show. Astonishingly they met the target, and she rehearsed it for eight hours, non-stop, and recorded it two days later. And, this being Piaf, her clown was no ordinary clown.

128: *Bravo pour le clown!* (Bravo for the clown!) (Henri Contet, Louiguy).
18 July: Columbia BF567, A-side.
18 April 1954: live in French television's *La joie de vivre d'Édith Piaf.*
4 January 1956: live, with English introduction at Carnegie Hall, New York.
Accompaniment: Robert Chauvigny & His Orchestra.

> A clown is my friend—a ridiculous clown whose name is written in capital letters. Not handsome for an empire—sadder than a hat! He drinks enormous laughter, and eats bravos [Contet's way of saying that he lives only for his work]. For your nose that lights up—Bravo! For the hair that they pluck out—Bravo! You munch plates whilst sitting on a water-jet. You gnaw glitter whilst twisted inside a barrel....Bravo! The loud applause rings in his ears—it robs him of his sorrows and empties his bottles. His unscrewed heart cannot sadden them—

they applaud for the life he missed out on. For your unfaithful wife—Bravo! And you wash the dishes—Bravo! Your life's a reproach that slaps you on the back. Your son thieves from you [*te fais les poches*] and *you* act the fool—Bravo!

Then comes the finale which, when Piaf performed the song on the television, saw the stage invaded with clowns and all manner of circus acts:

> The circus is deserted—it's no good laughing. My clown is locked up in a certain lunatic asylum. Success in a straitjacket—bravos in a padded cell! Hands that go crazy, and beat him with their song! *"I am King, and I rule—Bravo! I have laughs that bleed—Bravo! Come, let me be cheered—I've done my bit, throwing my wife from the top of the marquee! Bravo!"*

The day after recording this song, Piaf's manager, Louis Barrier—the man she trusted more than any other—took matters into his own hands and checked her into a detox clinic, from which she emerged *almost* cured—sufficiently for her to continue with the Super-Circus tour. This proved a disaster. Because there would be children in the audience, she was requested not to sing any songs about hardship, lost love, prostitutes and death—effectively diminishing her repertoire. Halfway through, she was offered a small part in a film—playing a revolutionary in Sacha Guitry's *Si*

189

Versailles m'était conté, a sprawling epic telling the story of the building of the famous palace and featuring the largest cast of international names assembled thus far in a European film: Gérard Philipe, Tino Rossi, Brigitte Bardot, Claudette Colbert, Orson Welles were but the top of a very prestigious iceberg. Shooting on the production had begun on 6 June, and would wrap on 18 September, with Piaf's segment—she played "une femme du peuple" [woman of the people]—completed towards the end of the schedule.

129: *Le "ça ira"* (It'll be all right!) (Arr. Jean Françaix)
September: soundtrack recording for the film, *Si Versailles m'était conté.* (*GB: Royal Affairs In Versailles*).
13 December: Columbia BF 619, A-side.
Accompaniment: Robert Chauvigny & His Orchestra. Choir: Marguerite Murcier. The B-side of this recording features Jacques Pills singing *Le Grisbi,* from the film *Touchez-pas au grisbi.*
The "Ça ira" was the emblematic anthem of the French Revolution, first heard in 1790. There have been several versions over the years, some extremely vulgar. Director Sacha Guitry brought in the neo-classical composer Jean Francaix (1912-97) to score the film, and arrange this much-moderated version of the piece for Piaf.

It'll be all right! The aristocrats—string them up [*à la lanterne*! The aristocrats—we're going to hang them! For three-hundred years now they've promised to give us bread—for three-hundred years

190

now they've been having parties and financing whores! For three-hundred years now we [the people] have been crushed! Enough of their lies and speeches—we no longer want to die of hunger! It's all right!....For three-hundred years now they've been at war—to the sound of fife and drum, leaving us to die of misery! That can't last for ever! For three-hundred years now they take our men and treat us like beasts of burden! This can't last for ever! It's all right!....Punishment is on its way to you, for the people are regaining their rights!...It's over, gentlemen kings! We no longer need our own heads—we can have yours instead! Because we're the ones making the laws! It'll be all right! The aristocrats—string them up! The aristocrats—we're going to hang them!

There were two trios of songs at this time. The first was courtesy of Michel Emer and saw all three songs released the following year. The second was a collaboration between Piaf and Marc Heyral, who earlier had provided her with *Le Noël de la rue* and *N'y vas pas Manuel*, which did not fare quite so well. Two of the songs were archived and have yet to surface, while such was Piaf's power that the one scheduled for release (*L'éffet que tu me fais*) was also archived because it had been written with Jacques Pills in mind—after just seventeen months of marriage, "Mr. Piaf" was already on his way out.

130: *Et moi…*(And me…) (Michel Emer).
11 December: Columbia BF 600, A-side.
Accompaniment: Robert Chauvigny & His Orchestra.

> I didn't know how to pray—I wasn't thus inclined
> [*je n'avais pas la manière*]. If I did, occasionally, it
> was when I was hungry. Now, every morning I
> make the same prayer: "*Give me today his daily
> love!*" Trees cannot live without rain. Flowers
> cannot sprout [*éclore*] during the night. Without
> water, goldfish would no longer breathe. And me,
> without you I am lost! Without breeze, the sailboat
> would not move forwards. Without music, no one
> would dance any more. Without the sunshine, birds
> would no longer sing. And me, without you I am
> lost! I have neither faith nor law. When you're far
> away from me everything is gloomy and joyless,
> without you. Without you, everything seems
> bitter—the earth is a hell! You're more necessary to
> me than air! To become golden, the cornfields need
> light. To be worshipped, God needs mysteries.
> Men's hearts would no longer beat without love.
> And me, without you I am lost!

131: *Soeur Anne* (Sister Anne) (Michel Emer)*
11 December: Columbia BF 600, B-side.
11 January 1955: live, Geneva. Released posthumously.
Accompaniment: Robert Chauvigny & His Orchestra.
Choir: Raymond Saint-Paul.

* According to Christian apocryphal tradition, the Soeur Anne referred to in the song is the mother of the Virgin Mary, and thus the grandmother of Jesus. At the beginning of each verse, Piaf asks Saint Anne to look into the future, and poses: *"Sister Anne, do you see nothing coming?"*

She responds:

> I see armed soldiers, prepared to die and kill. Everywhere, I see only tears—the world seeming to get used to it. I see hate covering the horizon, more violent than the plague—men tearing each other apart, hating each other. Borders, machine-guns, prisons. Love, with nothing left to do, has just turned around and left. On earth, it was lonely, and love needs love!....I see children without their mother. I see parents without children, farmers without lands, lands without farmers. I see big empty houses—big empty spaces inside houses. People with livid faces, walking around without singing. Men who try to smile—women with fearful expressions. Old people who no longer know how to laugh—young people who are already old....

Saint Anne then predicts the Second Coming:

> I see a great light which seems to come from far off. I see a child and his mother. My God, they're so, so far away!....Then they're approaching the earth. The

child has grown. I see him! He's come to share our sorrows. Already, he's carrying his Cross. Soon, his divine wrath will chase away the demon for ever. Life, pity and love will soon return to the earth!

132: *N'y vas pas Manuel* (Michel Emer)
11 December: Columbia BF 596, A-side.
Accompaniment: Robert Chauvigny & His Orchestra.

> He was only ten years old but he was already a brawler—insolent, filled with violence. He wanted to be a tough man, like in the movies, and above all he wanted to be gang-leader [*menait la danse*]. He spent his days running through the streets, thinking only about fighting, only of punching. His despairing mother, who couldn't take it anymore, spent all of her time pleading: *"Don't go, Manuel! Don't go! There are things in life one doesn't do! Later, you'll regret it! Don't go! When the day finally comes when you understand you shouldn't have done that, it will be too late! Don't go!"*

Thus Manuel becomes a man, and obviously has not taken his mother's advice, though as with *Elle a dit*, when tragedy ensues, we do not get to know how he dies.

> He's now a Monsieur who doesn't like detectives [*les agents*]—doesn't want them meddling in his affairs. To have a good life one needs lots of money

194

and there are thirty-six ways to do this. Work's boring and tiresome. He manages very well without making much of an effort. His wife, whom he spoils a lot but who doesn't ask for much, tells him each evening when he goes out: *"Don't go, Manuel!"*....But Manuel doesn't give a damn about all their sermons. Tonight he's got a big job on. It will be his last one, for tomorrow morning he's off to start a new life in America. With a flexible and light step, he quietly leaves for the place where they [his partners in crime] all meet. Everything is quiet, yet he vaguely hears a voice coming from who knows where. *"Don't go, Manuel...watch out, Manuel! Be careful!....Oh, Manuel!"*

133: *Il y avait vraiment des choses* (Truly, there were things) (Marc Heyral, Edith Piaf).
13 December: archived. No other details.
Accompaniment: Robert Chauvigny & His Orchestra.

134: *Ça y est, c'est arrivé!* (That's it, it's happening!) (Marc Heyral, Edith Piaf).
13 December: archived. No other details.
Accompaniment: Robert Chauvigny & His Orchestra.

135: *L'effet que tu me fais* (The effect you have on me) (Marc Heyral, Edith Piaf).
14 December: archived, released posthumously.
Accompaniment: Robert Chauvigny & His Orchestra.

There are people who know how to express the magnitude of their sentiments. For myself, it's not so easy. It's a question of temperament. I can't say what effect you have on me. It's true, you have a funny effect—it begins here, goes by there, and leaves! I ask myself where [it goes to]—that I don't know—but it comes back and does it again! There's only one remedy to calm this—it's when you take me in your arms! My line of fate is within *your* hand, my happy days within your eyes. You could well say that life has such wonderful moments that I ask if heaven, whatever they say, is better than here! If only I could explain what effect you have on me!....If you want to know my impression, our love's a little white. White is fine, but it soon gets dirty! So I'm very cautious. I can't explain the effect you have on me!....Do you really think there's a chance of us loving each other and being happy? There are so many people in life who want to be in love! You have ways of looking at me. Truly, there's no need for you to speak. And if I have the effect on you that you have on me—well, it's true, we have a funny effect on each other!

136: *Encore un verre!* (Let's have another drink!) (Edith Piaf, Marguerite Monnot.

December: tape recording, archived. No other details.

Like Piaf's earlier songs written for Yves Montand, this one makes little sense—and is bland, compared to her other compositions at around this time. She eventually gave it to Marguerite Monnot's actor-singer husband Paul Péri (1924-94), who recorded it in 1955.

> Let's have another drink, to the health of the girl who left me! Let's form a choir and sing about my sorrow, my heart! Here's to your health, you lovers, and to those of you who are married! I daren't go home, for I need to go to bed for a long time! I can't live without her! Yesterday, she told me once again, "*If you leave me, I'll kill myself!*" Let's have another drink, to the health of the girl who left me!....She was very orderly, and she's taken everything with her. She says it's my fault, but that's not true. Let's have another drink!

137: *Quand je l'embrasse* (When I kiss her) (Edith Piaf, Louiguy).
December: tape recording, archived.
December: Columbia SRCF 123, A-side, recorded by Jacques Pills.
Accompaniment: Robert Chauvigny & His Orchestra.

Simone Berteaut, who later claimed to have been Piaf's half-sister, recalled of her next, so-called "wedding song":

> Piaf's marriage was a disaster from the start. She recorded the song then dropped it from her repertoire—having never performed it on stage. She

recorded it again the following year—thinking that doing so on Valentine's Day might bring her luck. It didn't, so she dropped it again. Then, when Pills was out of the picture—though it would take a couple more years for her to get him out of her hair completely—she put it into her repertoire, and it remained there for several years *until* her divorce came through!

138: *Heureuse* (Happy) (René Rouzaud, Marguerite Monnot).
24 December: archived, released posthumously. *
14 February 1954: Columbia BF 599, B-side. **
January 1955: live, Paris Olympia. ***
13 January 1957: live in French & English, Carnegie Hall, New York. ****
* Accompaniment: Robert Chauvigny & His Orchestra. Choir: Marguerite Murcier.
** Organ accompaniment unknown. The label states the Murcier Choir, but this is an error.
*** Accompaniment: Robert Chauvigny & His Orchestra.
**** Chauvigny Orchestra augmented by in-house choir.

Happy as can be—in spite of everything. Happy! It must be so—I want it, my love, for we two! Happy finally to have a part of heaven—in your eyes, in your arms! Happy as can be—no matter where, through you! For better or worse, we share it. They call it loving for ever, but for me the worst would be to lose the best, for good. Being close to you, weeping with joy, happy as everything! Happy, tomorrow, about all and nothing, so long as you're there! You'll see! Happy until the end, through you!

The close of this year saw Piaf "flipping the coin", as she put it. Charles Aznavour recalled:

> She declared that American singers had been stealing her songs for years—having forgotten that *she* had purloined *Jézébel*—therefore the time had come for her to steal a few of theirs. And of course, once she did this, those songs became her own, they became definitive Piaf!

139: *Johnny, tu n'es pas un ange* (Johnny, you're no angel) (Francis Lemarque, Richard Stein, Les Paul).
24 December: longer version, released posthumously.
26 December: Columbia BF 596, B-side.
Accompaniment: Robert Chauvigny & His Orchestra.
Backing singers unknown.
A Romanian folk-song, *Sanie cu zurgălăi*, written by Richard Stein and Liviu Deleanu in 1936. *Johnny Is The Boy For Me*, the English adaptation by Paddy Roberts and Marcel Stellman was recorded by Les Paul and Mary Ford early in 1953, with Paul (1916-2009) boasting that he had composed the music. Stein successfully sued him for plagiarism, by which time the Piaf recording had been released. Thus his name appears on the sheet-music and the

label. In the Paul/Ford version, the lyrics of the chorus are replaced by Eastern European musical instruments. Francis Lemarque (1917-2002) was a singer-songwriter best known at the time for *À Paris* and *Le petit cordonnier*, which as *The Little Shoemaker* was a hit for Petula Clark. His lyrics have nothing to do with the original or the English ones.

Johnny, you're no angel! Don't think it bothers me! Day and night I think about you. You, do you remember me—when it suits you, and when morning comes and you fall asleep on my sorrow? Johnny…if you were more gallant I would love you just as much! Johnny, you're no angel…If you wake me up in the night it's to tell me you're bored, that you need a spare life [aka: to find someone else], but when morning comes, you're [still] sleeping on my sorrow! Johnny, you're no angel—but what does that change between us? The man will always know how to find all the women in the world to sing his praises, and as soon as he tires of them they're soon forgotten. Truly, you [men] are no angels! Johnny—since the world was born, we have to forgive them all! Ah, Johnny!

With Jacques Pills.

"La femme du people" in *Si Versailles m'était conté*.

With Michel Emer
in *La joie de vivre*.

1954

Much of the first half of this year was spent in and out of rehabilitation clinics—often for just one week at a time, so as not to interfere with Piaf's schedule, though this did her far more bad than good, and saw some of the major theatres refusing to hire her. The Olympia music-hall had been renovated and taken over by Bruno Coquatrix (1910-79), who would become a close friend of Piaf—though she was not very keen on him just now, as the gala test-opening had seen him engage Lucienne Delyle to headline and not her, with Gilbert Bécaud as her *vedette-américaine* (the artiste secondary to the *vedette*, who closed the first half of the show). The actual opening was scheduled to take place on 5 April, when Delyle was again selected instead of Piaf—in view of her drug and alcohol-related problems, Coquatrix had not wished to take the risk of her "bailing out" halfway through her season. The Alhambra had every confidence in her and she opened here in an extended season in February, where she introduced two new songs—one which became one of her most celebrated, the other forgotten.

140: *La goualante du pauvre Jean* (The ballad of poor Jean) (René Rouzaud, Marguerite Monnot).
16 February: Columbia BF 599, A-side.
9 October: live in the musical short, *Sur toute la gamme*, introduced by Maurice Chevalier.
4 January 1956: live in French & English, Carnegie Hall, New York.

23 September 1956: live, with English introduction, on *The Ed Sullivan Show*.

Accompaniment: Robert Chauvigny & His Orchestra. Backing singers: his musicians.

Piaf was offered an English-language version of the song, *The Poor People of Paris*, by Jack Lawrence (1912-2009), whose *All Or Nothing At All* had given Frank Sinatra a Number 1 hit in 1943. The title came courtesy of Lawrence's misinterpretation of the title—the French words *pauvre Jean* (poor Jean) pronounced the same as *pauvre gens* (poor people). She denounced the lyrics (particularly the couplet: *Milk or water from the sink/ Make a true Parisian shrink/ Wine is all he'll ever drink/ And it worries me!*) as "beyond stupid", but praised the instrumental version by pianist Winifred Atwell which topped the UK charts for three weeks. Like some of Piaf's earlier songs, this one is written mostly in slang.

> Listen but for a moment to the ballad of poor Jean, who women didn't like. But don't forget, in life there's just one moral. Whether we are rich or penniless, without love we are nothing! He lived from day to day in silk and velvet, kipped in fine sheets. But don't forget—life means squat (*peau de balle*) when our heart is in hock *(au clou)*. Without love, we are nothing! He scoffed food with barons, boogied in parlours, guzzled grog (*les tafias*). But don't forget—nothing beats a beautiful girl who shares your stew! Without love, we are nothing! To

earn some dosh (*des picaillons*), he was a wicked scoundrel (*un méchant larron*), held in low esteem (*on le saluait bien bas*)....One day, he goes too far with his tricks (*on fait la pirouette*)—when we are behind bars (*derrière les verrous*) we are nothing without love! Listen well, young people! Make the best of your twenties—we only have them once! And don't forget—it's better to have a woman around your neck than a rope!....So there we go, good people: the ballad of poor Jean, which ends by telling you, "Love yourselves!"

141: *Au revoir* (Michel Emer)
16 February: Columbia, archived.
26 February: live recording, Alhambra, archived.
Accompaniment: Robert Chauvigny & His Orchestra.
Registered with Editions Paul Beuscher-Arpèges.
No other details.

On 3 April, Piaf appeared in the previously mentioned television special, *La joie de vivre*, the first of two (the other being in 1956). Almost a French version of Britain's *This Is Your Life*, the invited guests were Jacques Pills, Roland Avelis (whose gimmick was being billed as Le Chanteur Sans Nom—The Singer Without A Name), Piaf's actress friend Suzanne Flon, and songwriters Henri Contet, Michel Emer and Marguerite Monnot. This was followed by another spell in rehab, cut short by Piaf so that she could continue with the Super-Circus—a big mistake because this saw her re-entering the clinic at the end of July for almost a month, after which there was a lengthy period of recuperation which saw her almost back to her old self, the only thorn in her side—according to Simone Berteaut, Marlene Dietrich and other intimates —being her husband. Thus, three months after the end of the Super-Circus tour, she was able to re-enter the studio.

142: *Avec ce soleil* (With this generation) (Michel Philippe-Gérard, Jacques Larue).
20 October: (Version 1) Columbia BF 668, B-side.
25 November: (Version 2) Columbia BF 684, A-side. *
January 1955: live, Paris Olympia.
Accompaniment: Robert Chauvigny & His Orchestra.
A song which Piaf shared with Patachou, who released her version at the same time, on the B-side of *L'enfant de la balle*. Version 1 runs at 2: 20 while the Version 2 runs at 2:30 and has a different orchestral arrangement, and choir. Here, the term *avec ce soleil* has nothing to do with the sunshine. It refers to the present generation—the youth of today who the lyricist allegorises with the poppy and the cornflower—the symbols of hope, worn on either side of the Channel at remembrance events.

Today's generation: they didn't want to talk, to take life at a steady pace [*de boire la vie à petites goulées*] under the superb sky—along the riverbank, chewing a blade of grass. Wearing a pleated skirt and with a cocky attitude [*d'un air triomphant*], she looked at this beardless [*imberbe* = meaning that that he has not yet started shaving] young man, not much more than a child, who desired her. It would have taken almost nothing—perhaps a gesture from him, a smile from her—from him to say, "*Come!*" [Similarly] it would have taken nothing—perhaps a bird flapping its wings and flying to freedom over the factory roof, along the grey walls, the hills and forests, the neighbouring road and its grey cobblestones, rising to the sky, without bells, without weddings—to purify the love of these kids. But these were already two hardened children who believed that they only had grown-up words to say to each other—for whom life was already mercilessly crushed, whose hearts were indifferent, who no longer knew how to dream or laugh. And that day, along the riverbank, poppies and cornflowers awaited being plucked by a cruel hand [in other words, these youngsters may not have much of a future to look forward to].

143: *Sous le ciel de Paris* (Under the Paris sky) (Hubert Giraud, Jean Dréjac).
20 October: (Version 1) Columbia BF 668, A-side. *
23 November (Version 2) Columbia BF 703, A-side. **
4 January 1956: live in French & English, Carnegie Hall.
Accompaniment: Robert Chauvigny & His Orchestra.
Choir: Marguerite Murcier.
* Accordion: Marcel Azzola. ** Accordion: Marc Bonel.

Written in 1950, this was performed by Jean Bretonnière in Julien Duvivier's film, *Sous le ciel de Paris*, released the following year. There were several cover-versions prior to the Piaf recording, the most acclaimed one being that by Juliette Gréco, in whose repertoire it remained for over sixty years. Marcel Azzola (1927-2014) collaborated with some of the greatest names of the French music-hall, notably Gréco, Jacques Brel, Barbara and Yves Montand. Marc Bonel (1911-2002), had accompanied Piaf off and on during the late 1940s, mostly on the radio, and now became her regular accordionist. His wife, Danielle (1919-2012) was her closest confidante almost throughout the entirety of her career. Hubert Giraud (1920-2016) had previously worked with Django Reinhardt and Ray Ventura. Jean Dréjac (1921-2003) would become a Piaf regular, mostly adapting American songs into French.

A song floats under the Paris sky, born today in a boy's heart. Lovers walk under the Paris sky, their love built on the tune made for them. Under the Pont de Bercy sits a philosopher, two musicians, a few onlookers. Then until evening, under the Paris sky, thousands sing the anthem of the people enamoured of this old city. Perhaps trouble is brewing near Notre Dame, but in Paname everything gets sorted out.* A few rays of summer sunshine, a sailor's accordion—hope blossoms under the Paris sky! The joyful river flows under the Paris sky…It lulls the tramps and ne'er-do-wells to sleep. The Good Lord's birds come from all over the world to chat amongst themselves under the Paris sky. But the Paris sky has its own secret! For twenty centuries it's been enamoured of our Île Saint Louis!** When [the island] smiles at [the sky], it dresses in blue. When it rains in Paris, it's because [the sky] is unhappy. When [the sky] gets too jealous of the millions of lovers, it unleashes its rumbling thunder upon them. But the Paris sky isn't cruel for long. So that it may be forgiven it offers a rainbow!

* Paname—a slang word for Paris which owes its origins to the early 20th century, when Panama hats were all the rage.
** the Île Saint Louis, one of the two natural islands in the middle of the river, the other being the Île de la Cité, upon which stands Notre Dame.

144: *Mea culpa* (My fault) (Michel Rivgauche, Hubert Giraud).
28 October: Columbia BF 670, A-side.
Accompaniment: Robert Chauvigny & His Orchestra.
The song won this year's Grand Prix de la Chanson. There was a cover-version by Mouloudji. Michel Rivgauche (1923-2006) was another new addition to the Piaf clan—with his pencil-line moustache, she described him as "her personal baddie from the silent movies". In this one, having already sung about the leaden cross weighing her down, Piaf focuses her attention on her sins.

I sinned, by way of pride of having you all to myself, in the blink of an eye. My fault! I sinned ,by way of envy in giving myself to you—in giving you my life. My fault! Then, out of greed, illuminated by the glow of your eyes, I saw your mouth and felt grey, for I was drinking fire. I sinned by way of laziness when I knew your arms—cradle of my caresses. My fault! That those who have never sinned should throw the first stone at me—that those who have never loved should refuse me a prayer! I sinned by way of anger—against you, against me, against all the earth. My fault! I have sinned by way of lust, every evening within your arms. But my soul was pure. My fault! And then, by way of avarice I hid you deep inside my heart—to better adore you there with delight, safe from thieves. So, you see. I've sinned seven times just because of you. My fault! But if one day you asked me, my love, I would start all over again! My fault!

145: *Enfin le printemps!* (Spring, at last!) (René Rouzaud, Marguerite Monnot).
29 October: Columbia BF 670, B-side.
Accompaniment: Robert Chauvigny & His Orchestra.
The "Jules" here is not a man, but Parisian slang for *boyfriend*. Much of the lyric, where Piaf juxtaposes spring with a previous lover, is in *argot*. And if the song gives an impression of optimism, it ends with a warning—that if *this* boy does not want her, she will find another who does!

My boyfriend, take aim at this scoundrel falling into our arms! For some time we've awaited him like a bomb—here he is! Spring, all-abloom with lilacs, the return to dancing the *java*! Here he is, the thug with the roving eye, plugging his songs to the sound of the accordion! Listen to how he heckles all the throbbing hearts! Winter's playing a blinder [rough translation: *se tire des flutes*]. Spring, at last! Don't sulk! You'd be such an idiot to worry and fret, when a little revolutionary tune floats over all the earth! For you I took out my silk dress, my baubles, so that we can sleep on the grass, listening to the tinkling of the lilies-of-the-valley!....There's a crowd in the streets, bare-shouldered, following the fanfares—everyone's out on their balconies! It's Poets Day, and I'm hopelessly in love with you! It's making my head spin—Spring, at last! I go dizzy looking into your eyes! I'm all over the place [*je voltage dans du bleu*]! I'm seeing double, and that's better! So take aim up here at my heart that's flying like a kite. Catch it if you can, my love! My love's vanishing—Spring, at last!

146: *L'homme au piano* (The man on the piano) (Horst-Heinz Henning, Heinz Terningsohn, Jean-Claude Darnal).
26 November: Columbia BF 705, A-side.
Accompaniment: Robert Chauvigny (at the clavier) & His Orchestra.

The French adaptation of a German song, *Der Mann Am Klavier*, introduced by The Cornel Trio earlier in this year. Jean-Claude Darnal (1920-2011) was a singer-songwriter and actor who penned many hits for artistes as diverse as Piaf, Juliette Gréco, Petula Clark and Catherine Sauvage. His French adaptation, though melodically endearing, does not make much more sense than the German original (with its repetition of *"Give the man at the piano another beer!"*), and omits the middle section. Henning and Terningsohn (1920-98) were the same person.

Ask the man at the piano to knock out hammer-blows....to strike to his heart's content, right or wrong! I know his fingers are not made of wood, but when he breaks them we'll have them replaced! The main thing is that he plays non-stop as if on a fruit-machine, until he finishes. Perhaps your heart will hear a little of this racket, and then you'll understand that the piano's playing for you. I have to do my best to hunt the silent ghost! If the gentleman makes a noise it's not because I'm yelling at him to bang like he's deaf. He could never sound more fake than the words of the song that spoke of our love! Ask the man at the piano to knock out hammer-blows....to smash the love inside my head to pieces! Even if he only has one finger left and he taps [the keys] with his arms, I don't give a damn! The main thing is that he plays non-stop as if on a fruit-machine, until he finishes!

147: *Retour* (Return) (Georges Manet, Jean-Marie, Joe Heyne).

25 November: Columbia BF 684, B-side.

Accompaniment: Marc Herrand & His Orchestra.

Joe Heyne (1904-78) was a Belgian composer, so feted in his country that a Brussels park was named after him. Lyrically and musically, this song about a soldier's friend bidding him farewell as he goes home from the war, either on leave or wounded, is one of the most beautiful songs that Piaf recorded this year. Robert Chauvigny never explained why he refused to accompany her in the studio, and sadly she never performed it on the stage. In his place, Marc Herrand excels.

> You're going home, comrade, and for you peace will be reborn. Leave your gun and your grenades here. By extending our hands, we offer you hope. Think about us staying here at war—the quiet nights beloved of your heart. And go tell my mother and father that I'll be back, perhaps at Christmas. Don't tell them about the Front. Don't talk about the fire—and lie when you have to lie. Tell them we were all singing and raising the glass of farewell when you had to leave. You're going home, comrade…

Piaf finished off this year with a cameo appearance in the film *French Cancan*, a Franco-Italian musical production scripted and directed by Jean Renoir, with Françoise Anoul,

213

Jean Gabin and Maria Félix in the lead roles. It tells the story of the development of the scandalous routine, and its introduction at the Moulin Rouge. The other cameos included Patachou, André Claveau, while Cora Vaucaire provided the voice for the actress (Anna Amendola) playing the character Esther Georges—her song, *La complainte de la Butte*, was one of the biggest hits of the decade. Piaf portrayed the *revencharde* singer, Eugénie Buffet (1866-1934).

148: *Sérénade du pavé* (Pavement serenade) (Jean Varney). 13 December: soundstage recording at the Joinville Studios in Paris. The final refrain was used in the film, while the complete version of the song was released posthumously. Accompaniment: Georges Van Parys & His Orchestra.
The song was written in 1895, recorded *a cappella* by Buffet soon afterwards, and committed to shellac in 1929: it was included in the soundtrack of Renoir's film, *La Chienne*. Buffet, who believed the only way to sing about prostitutes was to play out the actual role, was a "camp-follower", traipsing across the North African desert after *legionnaires*. Amy Jolly, Gary Cooper's love-interest in the 1931 film *Morocco*, played by Marlene Dietrich, was based on her. In the song Buffet feigned the role of a beggar singing outside a rich woman's home, adding insult to injury by addressing her familiarly as *tu*, and not *vous*.

If I'm singing under your window like a gallant troubadour and if I want you to make an appearance it's not about love! I don't care if you're beautiful, a duchess or a doe-eyed courtesan—or whether you're washing dishes as long as you throw me a couple of *sous*. Be good, dear stranger, for whom I often sing! Your donation's welcome! Show me charity! Before me, your presence is welcome! You see, I don't care about love. That's only beautiful in songs. If I become rich one day, I'll be loved anyway. I'll become a chatelaine—at least if I have a castle—instead of an old woollen sweater and boots that let in water! Be good, dear stranger! But your window stays closed, and the two *sous* don't fall [at my feet]. Therefore I'm waiting for a little something. Throw me whatever you like—money, dry bread, old rags! Everything will make me pleased with you, and I'll pray for God to protect you a little more than he has protected me! Be good, dear stranger!

By this time, Piaf was more settled than she had been for some time, though she would have some way to go before ridding herself of her drink and drug-addictions—and of a husband who was by now surplus to requirements. Then, quite out of the blue—having been rejected earlier in the year—her career attained unprecedented heights when her manager, Louis Barrier, secured her an extended contract with the most famous and prestigious of all the French music-halls, the Paris Olympia.

With Marc & Danielle Bonel

With Michel Rivgauche.

In Montreuil, during the Super-Circus tour.

In *French Cancan*.

Discography

Unless otherwise stated, all are 78 rpm shellac recordings.

Columbia DF 3152
La vie en rose / Un refrain courait dans la rue

Columbia DF 3069
Adieu mon coeur / Le chant du pirate

Columbia DF 3170
*C'est merveilleux / Margotan va t'a l'iau *
   * sung by Les Compagnons de la Chanson

Columbia DFX 246 (30cm/12-inch)
Mariage / Un homme comme les autres

Columbia DCX 76
*Les trois cloches / Perrine était servant *
  *sung by Les Compagnons de la Chanson

Decca MB 8180
Le geste / Monsieur Ernest a reussi

Decca MB 8181
Si tu partais / Les cloches sonnent

Decca OMB 15 002 (30cm/12-inch)
Sophie / Une chanson à trois temps

Decca MB 20 242
Les vieux bateaux / Monsieur X

Decca MEI 20 260
Amour du mois de mai / Cousu de fil blanc

Columbia BF 128
Bal dans ma rue / Le prisonnier de la tour

Columbia BF 133
Paris / Pour moi toute seule

Columbia BF 189
Les amants de Paris / Monsieur Lenoble *
* labelled as *T'as pas profité de ta chance*)

Columbia DF 3244 (re-isssue of BF 189 with title change)
Les amants de Paris /Monsieur Lenoble

Columbia DFX 248 (30 cm/12-inch)
Pot pourri de chansons: Le petit homme / Je m'en fous pas mal / Un refrain courait dans la rue / Qu'as tu fait, John?/ Il a chanté

Columbia DF 3283
Il pleut (Version 2) / *Dany*

Columbia BF 265
Pleure pas / L'orgue des amoureux

Columbia BF 311
Tous les amoureux chantent / Le ciel est fermé

Columbia BF 306
Hymne à l'Amour / La petite Marie

Columbia BF 319
La Fête continue / C'est d'la faute

Columbia BF 330
C'est un gars / Il y avait

Columbia USA 38948
La Vie En Rose (English version) / *The Three Bells*

Columbia USA 39027
Hymn To Love / Simply A Waltz

Columbia USA 39135
My Lost Melody / Autumn Leaves

Columbia USA 39211
Don't Cry / Chante-moi (Darling Sing To Me)

Columbia USA 39320
Cause I Love You / I Shouldn't Care

Columbia BF 370
Demain, il fera jour / Avant l'heure

Columbia BF 371
Du matin jusqu'au soir / Rien de rien

Columbia BFX 34 (12-inch)
Chanson bleue / C'est toi (with Eddie Constantine)

Columbia BF 372
*Petite, si jolie * /Si, si, si* (with Eddie Constantine
* sung by Eddie Constantine

Columbia BF 375
La valse de l'amour / L'homme que j'aimerai

Columbia BFX 34 (12-inch)
*Chanson bleue / C'est toi (*with Eddie Constantine)

Columbia USA FL 9535 (10-inch vinyl album)
Edith Piaf: Hits from *La p'tite Lili:*
1: *Avant l'heure / Demain il fera jour / Rien de rien / Du matin jusqu'au soir / L'homme que j'aimerai / La valse de l'amour / C'est toi * / Si, si, si *￼* (*With Eddie Constantine)

Columbia BF 386
Chante-moi / Une enfant

Columbia BF 411
Plus bleu que tes yeux / Je hais les dimanches

Columbia BF 419
La rue aux chansons / Jezebel

Columbia BF 429
Padam, padam / La chanson de Catherine

Columbia BF 436
À l'enseigne de la Fille Sans Coeur / Telégramme

Columbia FS 1008 (10-inch vinyl album)
La vie en rose / C'est de la faute / La fête Continue / Hymne à l'Amour / Je hais les dimanches/ Padam, padam / Plus bleu que tes yeux / Jezebel

Columbia BF 464
C'est toi (solo version) */ Le Noël de la rue*

Columbia BF 491
Je t'ai dans la peau / Au bal de la chance

Columbia BF 496
Ça gueule ça, Madame (with Jacques Pills) */ Tous mes rêves passes* (sung by Jacques Pills)

Columbia BF 567
Bravo pour le clown! / Les amants de Venise

Columbia BF 600
Et moi... / Soeur Anne

Columbia 33 FS 1014 (10-inch vinyl album)
*Je t'ai dans la peau / Telégramme / Du matin jusqu'au soir
Monsieur et Madame / Mon ami m'a donné / Chante-moi /
Noêl de la Rue / Au bal de la chance*

Columbia Masterworks USA A-1812 (7-inch vinyl EP)
*Notre Dame de Paris / Noël De La Rue / A l'enseigne de La
Fille Sans Coeur / Au bal de la chance*

Columbia ESRF 1007 (7-inch vinyl EP)
Edith Piaf et Tino Rossi: *Deux petits chaussons!*
Deux petits chaussons (TR) / *Pour un rêve d'amour* (TR) /
Pour qu'elle soi jolie ma chanson (EP/JP) / *Bravo pour le
clown* (EP)

VOX (6) USA VIP 30.000 (7-inch vinyl EP)
Edith Piaf Sings: *L'accordéoniste / Le fanion de la Légion /
Je n'en connais pas la fin / De l'autre côté de la rue*

Columbia: FS 1021 (10-inch vinyl album)
Le bel indifférent

Columbia BF 589
Les croix / Pour qu'elle soi jolie ma chanson (with Jacques
Pills)

Columbia BF 596
N'y vas pas, Manuel / Johnny, tu n'es pas un ange

Columbia BF 599
La goualante du pauvre Jean / Heureuse

Columbia 33 FS 1031 (10-inch vinyl album)
Edith Piaf rencontre Charles Trenet: *Jean et Martine* (EP) / *Les olivettes* (CT) / *Les croix* (EP) /*Chanson pour Noël* (CT) / *Pour qu'elle soit jolie ma chanson* (EP/JP) / *Bouquet de joie* (CT) / *Je t'ai dans la peau* (EP) / *Font-Romeu* (CT)/ *Au bal de la chance* (EP) / *Printemps à Rio* (CT)

Columbia BF 619
Le "ça ira" / Le grisbi (sung by Jacques Pills)

Columbia BF 668
Sous le ciel de Paris / Avec ce soleil

Columbia ESRF 1022 (7-inch vinyl)
La goualante de pauvre Jean / Heureuse / Soeur Anne / Johnny, tu n'es pas un ange

Columbia ESRF 1023 (7-inch vinyl)
Padam, padam / Jézébel / Mariage / Les amants de Venise

Columbia BF 670
Mea culpa / Enfin le printemps!

Columbia BF 684
Avec ce soleil / Retour

Columbia BF 703

Sous le ciel de Paris / Un grand amour qui s'achève *

*details of this song will appear in *Volume Three* of this series.

Columbia BF 705

L'homme au piano / Retour

Columbia CTX 40367 (12-inch vinyl album)

Mes premières chansons: Vol. 27: Un homme comme les autres; Il a chanté; Dany; Chanson bleue; N'y vas pas Manuel; Et moi; Tous les amoureux chantent; La valse de l'amour; L'effet que tu me fais; **Elle a dit***; Monsieur et Madame; Chante-moi; Jean et Martine; Un grand amour qui s'achève*

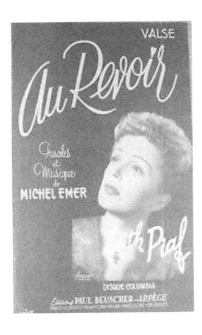

Songs

Songs marked * were written/co-written by Edith Piaf

Adieu mon coeur (2)
À l'enseigne de la Fille Sans Coeur (109)
All My Love (78)
Amour du mois de mai (37)
Au bal de la chance (114)
Au revoir (141)
Autumn Leaves (80)
Avant l'heure (91)
Avec ce soleil (142)
Bal dans ma rue (51)
Boléro (41)
Bravo pour le clown! (128)
Ça gueule ça, Madame (115) *
Cause I Love You (86) *
Ça y est, c'est arrive (134) *
Céline (13)
C'est de la faute (70) *
C'est merveilleux (4)
C'est pour ça (24)
C'est toi [1] (with Eddie Constantine) (96) *
Cest toi [2] (solo version) (107) *

Monsieur Lenoble (39)

Monsieur X (35)

My Lost Melody [1] (52)

My Lost Melody [2] (79)

My Lost Melody [3] (82)

Notre Dame de Paris (118)

N'y vas pas Manuel (132)

Padam, padam (103)

Paris (54)

Petite, si jolie (95) *

Pleure pas (58)

Plus bleu que tes yeux (101)

Pot pourri: Le petit homme/ Je m'en fous pas mal/ Un refrain courait dans la rue/ Qu'as tu fait, John? (42)

Pour moi toute seule (49)

Pour qu'elle soit jolie ma chanson (with Jacques Pills) (116) *

Quand je l'embrasse (137) *

Quand je te vois danser (15) *

Qu'as-tu fait, John? (23)

Retour (147)

Rien de rien (93)

Sérénade du pave (148)

Sérénade Florentine (21)

Simply A Waltz (76)

Si, si, si (with Eddie Constantine) (92)

Si tu partais (30)

Soeur Anne (131)

Sophie (32) *

Sous le ciel de Paris (143)
Télégramme (110)
The Three Bells (74)
Tous les amoureux chantent (57)
Tous mes rêves passes (111) *
Tu n'as pas besoin de mes rêves (56) *
Une chanson à trois temps (33)
Une enfant (98)
Un homme comme les autres (26) *
Un refrain courait dans la rue (6) *
What Can I Do? (61) *
Why Come Crying To Me? (117) *
You're Too Dangerous, Cheri (48) *

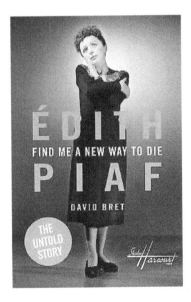

Made in the USA
Las Vegas, NV
17 December 2024